AROUND Seattle WITH KIDS

by Beth Taylor

Fodor's Travel Publications
New York • Toronto • London • Sydney • Auckland

www.fodors.com

CREDITS

Writer: Beth Taylor
Series Editor: Karen Cure
Editor: William Travis
Editorial Production: Marina J. Padakis
Production/Manufacturing: Robert Shields

Design: Fabrizio La Rocca, *creative director;*
Tigist Getachew, *art director*
Illustration and Series Design: Rico Lins, Keren Ora
Admoni/Rico Lins Studio

ABOUT THE WRITER

After spending a decade writing for the *Orlando Sentinel,*
Beth Taylor swapped her sunscreen for raingear and headed
off to the great Northwest. When she's not writing features
for *Seattle Magazine, Eastside Journal,* and the *Seattle
Times,* she likes nothing better than exploring the nooks
and crannies of Seattle with her favorite adventurers, hus-
band Scott and daughter Molly.

ISBN 0-676-90199-9
ISSN 1537-5552
First Edition

IMPORTANT TIPS

Although all prices, opening times, and other details in this
book are based on information supplied to us at press time,
changes occur all the time in the travel world, and Fodor's
cannot accept responsibility for facts that become outdat-
ed or for inadvertent errors or omissions. So always confirm
information when it matters, especially if you're making a
detour to visit a specific place.

SPECIAL SALES

Fodor's Travel Publications are available at special dis-
counts for bulk purchases for sales promotions or premiums.
Special editions, including personalized covers, excerpts of
existing guides, and corporate imprints, can be created in
large quantities for special needs. For more information,
contact your local bookseller or Special Markets, Fodor's
Travel Publications, 280 Park Avenue, New York, NY 10017.
Inquiries from Canada should be directed to your local
Canadian bookseller or sent to Random House of Canada,
Ltd., Marketing Dept., 2775 Matheson Boulevard East,
Mississauga, Ontario L4W 4P7. Inquiries from the United
Kingdom should be sent to Fodor's Travel Publications, 20
Vauxhall Bridge Road, London, England SW1V 2SA.

PRINTED IN THE UNITED STATES OF AMERICA
10 9 8 7 6 5 4 3 2 1

COUNTDOWN TO GOOD TIMES

GET READY, GET SET!

Everyone knows that organizing a family's schedule is a full-time job. Pickups, drop-offs, school, parties, after-school activities—everyone off in their own direction. Of course, it's an organizer's dream, but a scheduling nightmare. Spending time together shouldn't be another thing to have to figure out.

We know what's it's like to try to find good places to take your children or grandchildren. Sometimes it's tough to change plans when you suddenly hear about a kid-friendly event; besides, a lot of those events end up being crowded or, worse, sold out. It's also hard to remember places you read about in a newspaper or magazine, and sometimes just as hard to tell from the description what age group they're geared to. There's nothing like bringing a "grown-up" 12-year-old to an activity that's intended for his 6-year-old sister. Of course, if you're visiting Seattle, it's even harder to figure out the best things to do with your kids before you even get there. That's where we come in.

What you'll find in this book are 68 ways to have a terrific couple of hours or an entire day with your children or your grandchildren. We've scoured the city, digging out activities your kids will love—from the dazzling undersea life in the Seattle Aquarium to the birds and wildlife at Discovery Park. The best part is that it's stress-free, uncomplicated, and easy for you. Open the book to any page and find a helpful description of a kid-friendly attraction, with age ratings to make sure it's right for your family, smart tips on visiting so that you can get the most out of your time there, and family-friendly eats nearby. The address, telephone number, open hours, and admission prices are all there for your convenience. We've done the work, so you don't have to.

Naturally you'll still want to keep an eye out for seasonal events that fit your family's interests, from the landing of the pirates at Alki Beach the weekend after the 4th of July to the Milk Derby Races on Green Lake shortly afterward. Back-to-back festivals, farmers' markets, and parades fill the summer months. Get a taste of Northwest cuisine at Bite of Seattle, the region's biggest food festival, held in mid-July at Seattle Center. Throughout July and August, Seafair, a celebration of pirates and the region's seafaring past, stages a variety of events including a nighttime downtown Torchlight Parade and hydroplane races on Lake Washington. Seattle's biggest bash is Bumbershoot, a festival in honor of the upcoming rain season. Held at Seattle Center over Labor Day weekend, the festival presents a menagerie of spectacles from stilt-walking spiderwomen and audience-participation drum-beating to squealing kids racing through a giant fountain and acrobats scaling the Space Needle.

The day-after-Thanksgiving brings the Bon Marche Holiday Parade followed later that day by the Westlake Center Tree-Lighting Celebration, kicking off a season of downtown festivities including free rides on an antique carousel at Westlake Park. The annual SAM Lights Up!, a multicultural holiday celebration at Seattle Art Museum, is a free night of lights, entertainment, and refreshments. Wintertime is arts season, bringing a full slate of music and theater for all ages.

WAYS TO SAVE MONEY

We list only regular adult, student (with I.D.), and kids' prices; children under the ages specified are free. It always pays to ask at the ticket booth whether any discounts are offered for a particular status or affiliation (but don't forget to bring your I.D.). Discounts are often available for senior citizens, AAA members, military personnel, and veterans, among others. Many attractions offer family memberships, generally good for one year of unlimited use for your family. These memberships sometimes allow you to bring a guest. Prices vary, but the memberships often pay for themselves, if you visit the attraction several times a year. Sometimes there are other perks: newsletters or magazines, members-only previews, and discounts at a gift shop, for parking, or for birthday parties or special events. If you like a place when you visit, you can sometimes apply the value of your one-day admission to a membership if you do it before you leave.

Look for coupons—which can often save you $2–$3 per person—everywhere from the local newspaper to a supermarket display to your pediatrician's office. In addition, sometimes groups of attractions get together and offer combination tickets, which are cheaper than paying for each one individually. One such bargain is CityPass, which can save you 50% off regular ticket prices at Woodland Park Zoo, the Museum of Flight, Pacific Science Center, Argosy Cruises Harbor Tour, Seattle Aquarium and, the Space Needle. It costs $33.50 for adults and $21.50 for children ages 4–13.

You can buy one at any of these destinations, or order it in advance online (www.citypass.com/seattle/index.html).

Also keep an eye out for attractions—mostly museums and other cultural destinations—that offer free or discounted admission one day a month, particular days of the week, or before or after a certain time. We've noted some in this book.

WHEN TO GO

With the exception of seasonal attractions, kid-oriented destinations are generally busiest when children are out of school—especially weekends, holidays, and summer—but not necessarily. Attractions that draw school trips can be swamped with clusters of sometimes-inconsiderate children tall enough to block the view of your preschooler. But school groups tend to leave by early afternoon, so weekdays after 2 during the school year can be an excellent time to visit museums, zoos, and aquariums. For outdoor attractions, it's good to visit after a rain, since crowds will likely have cleared out.

The hours we list are the basic hours, not necessarily those applicable on holidays. Some attractions are closed when schools are closed, but others add extra hours on these days. It's always best to check if you want to see an attraction on a holiday.

SAFETY

Obviously the amount of vigilance necessary will depend on the attraction and the ages of your kids. In crowded attractions, keep an eye on your children at all times, as their ages warrant. When you arrive, point out what the staff or security people are wearing, and find a very visible landmark to use as a meeting place, should you get separated. If you do split into groups, pick a time to meet. This will decrease waiting time, help you and your kids get the most out of your time there, and manage everyone's expectations.

FINAL THOUGHTS

Actually, this time it's yours, not ours. We'd love to hear what you or your kids thought about the attractions you visited. Have you found other places we should include? Send us your ideas via e-mail (c/o editors@fodors.com, specifying Around Seattle with Kids on the subject line) or write to us at Around Seattle with Kids, Fodor's Travel Publications, 280 Park Avenue, New York, NY 10017). We'll put your ideas to good use. In the meantime, have fun in the Emerald City!

—The Editors

ALKI BEACH PARK

When Seattlelites say they're going to "the beach," this is probably where they're headed. Two miles of wide, flat beach and views of Puget Sound, the mountains, and downtown Seattle make this a great spot to take even the youngest kids for sunning, digging, Frisbee-throwing, or—for the brave—a dip in the water, which is chilly on the hottest of days.

Skirting the West Seattle peninsula, the beach runs nearly the whole length of Alki Avenue, from Duwamish Head to Alki Point. Huddled in the middle of the park, sandy beaches invite budding castle-builders and people watching. The beach, however, has no lifeguards, so use caution if you decide to go swimming. Grassy areas on the western end provide a playful respite from the sands, and an idyllic spot for a picnic.

On low-tide days, start with a free walk, led by naturalists, along the shore (tel. 206/296–8359 for time and dates of walks). Kids can hunt for crabs, anemones, snails, and jellyfish

KEEP IN MIND When the kids tire of lounging on the sand, you can rent skates or bikes across the street at **Randy's Bike & Blade Rentals** (63rd Ave. S.W. & Alki Beach, tel. 206/923–1965). You can even rent four-seat go-carts, which cost $20 for an hour's ride along a wide, paved trail that winds along the beach.

1702 Alki Ave. S.W., West Seattle

 Free

Daily 4 AM–11:30 PM

206/684–4075

All ages

hiding among the rocks and shells in the tide pools. During high tide, give the kids a taste of what they would have seen at low tide by taking them to the sculpted tidepool on 63rd Avenue. The huge bronze octopus and the tile mural swimming with colorful sea creatures always amuse.

Alki Beach is also known as the "Birthplace of Seattle." It was here on a rainy November day in 1851 that the first settlers landed. A human-size replica of the Statue of Liberty and the Birthplace of Seattle monument, made of rock brought cross-country from Plymouth Rock, marks the spot where the Denny Party landed. The names of all the children—as young as 6 weeks old—who were among the party are inscribed on the monument. If you've peaked your child's curiosity of this historic event, walk up to the Log House Museum (3003 61st Ave. S.W., tel. 206/938–5293), where exhibits tell of the early settlers and the friendly Indians who helped them survive the first winter.

HEY KIDS! One of the first founders of Seattle named the city "New York Alki," after his hometown and an Indian word meaning "by and by." It was later renamed in honor of a famous local Indian chief named Seattle.

EATS FOR KIDS Kid-friendly restaurants and cafes line the blocks across the street from the water, many of them with outdoor seating. Settle in at **Spud Fish & Chips** (2666 Alki S.W., West Seattle, tel. 206/938–0606) for some deep-fried popcorn shrimp, among other seafood favorites, or try **Pegasus** (2758 Alki S.W., West Seattle, 206/932–4849) for pizza and pasta. You'll also find grills and picnic tables along the shore.

BAINBRIDGE ISLAND HISTORICAL MUSEUM

At the turn of the 20th century, whistling steamboats ferried people back and forth to Bainbridge Island across the Puget Sound for a nickel. Today, it costs a bit more, but it's worth it to spend an afternoon visiting this museum and getting a taste of this island's history.

The museum is housed in a restored one-room schoolhouse built in 1908, and you can almost feel the teacher's stern gaze as you creak across the wooden floor boards. Not to worry, though; the only one eyeing you is a volunteer docent, eagerly anticipating any questions you might have. Historic photos, memorabilia, and interpretive signs unveil some quirky tidbits about the island, such as why so many ring-necked pheasants live there. In keeping with its nautical theme, the museum also displays a collection of sea creatures from the island's very own beaches. Kids are sure to marvel at this array of specimens, including scallops, sand dollars, and sea urchins.

HEY KIDS!
Don't be surprised if you see a ring-necked pheasant hanging around the area near the museum. It's just Phil the Pheasant, who often drops by the McDonalds and taps on the windows until someone brings him some french fries. Phil is a descendant of birds brought to the island in the early 20th century.

KEEP IN MIND Nearby Bainbridge Gardens makes a great side trip, with 7 acres of colorful and exotic flowers, trees, and shrubs. Owner Junkoh Harui, a Japanese-American man whose family was interned during the WWII, also recreated a Japanese garden, dedicating it to his dad, who had originally started the garden from seeds brought over from Japan.

7650 N.E. High School Rd.,
Bainbridge Island

 $3 adults, $1 under 18

🕐 Th, Sa, and Su 1–4

☎ 206/842–2773

🚼 8 and up

No history of Bainbridge Island is complete without mentioning its ties to Japan. Kids will learn that in the late 1800s, Japanese immigrants came to work at Bainbridge's two lumber mills, which were busy processing the island's giant firs. By the early 1900s, the mills were declining and most Japanese residents had shifted to agriculture. They launched the area's prosperous strawberry industry. But the story isn't all happy. A moving display called "For the Sake of the Children" tells about the Japanese-Americans torn from their homes during World War II. Japanese-American citizens of Bainbridge Island were the first to be sent to internment camps. This exhibit, with pictures and letters from the camps, may be too powerful for little ones; for older children, it could prompt a healthy discussion of tolerance and racism.

Before you go, show the kids the bench-style wooden seats where schoolchildren sat 100 years ago. It will give them a whole new appreciation for their modern classrooms!

EATS FOR KIDS Restaurants and cafes dot the downtown area near the ferry dock. A favorite is **La Belle Saison** (278 Winslow Way E., tel. 206/780–4064), a reasonably priced sandwich shop that also serves salads and a special sandwich platters for kids. Sunday brunch is also a treat. For those with a sweet tooth, head down the street to **Blackbird Bakery** (210 Winslow Way E., tel. 206/780–1422) for one of Alice's delicious lavender sugar cookies.

BOEING TOUR

The Boeing factory is a big building. A *really* big building. It's so big, it's listed in the Guinness Book of World Records as the largest building in the world in terms of volume. That's because the biggest airplanes in the world are assembled here. The company has come a long way since 1916, when founder Bill Boeing decided he could make a better plane. By 1966, the company had to build this factory to accommodate its new jumbo jet, the 747.

Before you start your factory tour, you'll be treated to a fascinating fast-sequence movie in the guest center. Kids can watch workers scurry around at hyper-speed as they build a 747 from start to finish. Then you're off on a bus ride to the factory, where an enormous elevator whisks you up to a catwalk, above the workers and planes. From here, you can walk around the building, starting in the area where small plane sections are assembled and ending in the final assembly bays.

HEY KIDS! Just how big is the Boeing building? It's big enough to fit 911 NBA basketball courts or 75 football fields! In fact, the factory has four doors, and each one is as big as a football field. They have to be huge, so the jumbo jets can fit through them when they're ready to fly. And if you walked around the outside of the building, you would be pretty tired by the time you were done—it's more than 2 miles around!

 Paine Field, Everett

 $5 adults,
$3 under 16

800/464-1476

 M–F 9, 10, 11, 1, 2, and 3

8 and up; no one under 4' 2" allowed; children under 16 must be accompanied by adult

Retired Boeing volunteers conduct the tours with infectious enthusiasm. They pepper their narrative with lots of quirky facts that kids will remember long after they leave. For example, planes come equipped with enough wiring to wrap around the world three times. The factory contains so many lights—1 million of them—that no heat is needed to stave off those chilly Seattle winters.

Although the guides are lively enough to keep a child's attention, try to stay near the front of the group. The factory gets quite noisy, and it's hard to hear from the back. After your tour, you return to the bus for a drive past the paint hangars and the rows of planes awaiting delivery. When customers arrive to pay for their planes, they get a gold key in a velvet box. It doesn't really work, but if you've just spent $200 million on a 747, you probably want something to show for it.

GETTING THERE
From Seattle, take I-5 north to Exit 189, then take State Highway 526 West. After about 3 miles, you'll see signs to the tour center. Limited public transportation is available from Seattle (tel. 206/553-3000 for details).

EATS FOR KIDS Just a mile away, you can munch on a pie at **Alfy's Pizza** (8204 Mukilteo Spdwy, tel. 425/353-1778). At nearby Mukilteo ferry landing, try **Ivar's** (710 Front St., tel. 425/347-3648), a family institution since 1938, for fish 'n' chips or its legendary chowder.

BURKE-GILMAN TRAIL

S tretching from Fremont to Kenmore, the Burke-Gilman and connecting trails provide picture-postcard scenery and a variety of interesting stops no matter where you start. Its flat, paved trail and plenty of access points make it easy to walk, bike, or skate with kids in tow, and for a scenic mile or two, kids can unleash some of that energy stored up from a rainy day.

If you start on the Fremont side, be sure to take a side trip to see the statue of a one-eyed troll eating a real Volkswagen Bug. You're not likely to see a statue like this anywhere else in the universe. Fremont contains quite a few quirky anomalies, such as a row of aluminum people, dressed seasonally and waiting for the Interurban Trolley, and a bronze statue of Vladimir Lenin, left over from the old Soviet Union. All these statues are within a couple of blocks of the trail.

KEEP IN MIND Since your sharing the trail with bicyclists and joggers, remind kids to keep to the right and allow faster runners and bicyclists to pass safely.

HEY KIDS! If you walk through Marymoor Park, you may see a large area of land covered with small, carefully tended gardens. That's the Pea Patch garden, and it's for people who live in the city and don't have room in their yards for growing vegetables. For $40 a year, they can rent a plot of land and plant to their hearts' content. One day each year, all the Pea Patch gardeners get together and donate some of their veggies to the local food bank to help feed hungry kids and grown-ups.

From the north end of the Fremont Bridge, the trail meanders pleasantly along beautiful Lake Union. It follows an old railroad bed through lush grasslands and valleys, through the charming University of Washington campus, along Lake Washington. The trail then meets the Sammamish River Trail, ending up in Redmond, home of the Microsoft campus. Gas Works Park (see #52) is about 2 miles from the Fremont start of the trail. After winding through the UW campus, the path leads through the disabled-accessible Burke-Gilman Place Park, then up to Warren G. Magnuson Park and Matthews Beach Park, where kids can frolic on playgrounds or swim in Lake Washington.

If you start on the eastern end of the trail, the sprawling waterfront Marymoor Park (see #44) in Redmond holds unusual amenities including a banked velodrome bike-racing track, an artificial rock for climbing, and a historic windmill. You can't go inside the windmill, but it's a great place for snapshots!

EATS FOR KIDS Great picnic parks dot the Burke-Gilman Trail, so you'll have your choice of scenic lunch spots. If you start out in Fremont, you'll be within two blocks of a dozen or so great eating spots. The tasty Thai at **Fremont Noodle House** (3411 Fremont Ave., tel. 206/547–1550) or the savory pies at **Fremont Classic Pizzeria** (4307 Fremont Ave. N., tel. 206/548–9411) are bound to satiate hungry hikers.

BURKE MUSEUM OF NATURAL HISTORY AND CULTURE

64

Dem bones, dem bones—you'll find plenty of them on display here. Amazing creatures stomped around Seattle millions of years ago, and this museum displays a variety of exhibits dedicated to these specimens. From dinosaur eggs and fossils as old as 500 million years to an allosaurus, the only real dinosaur skeleton found in the Northwest, children have lots to see and explore.

The museum goes to great lengths to appeal to junior scientists, such as by handing out "time cards" to kids, which can be stamped at kiosks throughout the museum's core exhibit, "Life and Times of Washington State." At each kiosk, kids can press a button for a short, lively video presentation on what was going on in Washington at various times. When the card is full, it gives a chronological account of how the state has changed in the last 500 million years. Budding rock collectors will want to gravitate to the Volcanic Rock & Mineral Display, with its fiery geodes, amethysts, and an amazing "picture agate" that looks like it's engraved with a seascape.

HEY KIDS! Did you know that 500 million years ago the whole state was underwater? Then about 65 million years ago, the land under the ocean started moving and cracking, causing lots of volcanoes to blow their tops and spew out lava. All this activity gradually formed the Cascade Mountains and built up the land until it was above sea level. And that's why you're standing on dry land today!

N.E. 45th St. and 17th Ave. N.E., University of Washington campus

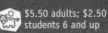 $5.50 adults; $2.50 students 6 and up

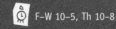 F–W 10–5, Th 10–8

206/543–5590

6 and up

On the lower floor, Pacific Rim cultures—Korean, Lao, Chinese, Japanese, Samoan, Hawaiian, Filipino and Native American—come to life through interactive exhibits with lots of buttons for kids to press. Children are invited to draw and write about their own families for future visitors to enjoy. Although kids as young as 2 enjoy pushing the buttons and looking at the dinosaurs, the only section really targeted to preschoolers is the Discovery Lab, tucked away just off the dinosaur area, where you and your toddlers can work puzzles and play with plastic dinosaurs. Around the perimeter, older kids can peer through microscopes at dinosaur bones and play science games on the computer.

A couple of hours is plenty of time to see this museum. It's just the right size to stimulate little minds without overwhelming them. Special events and programs are held throughout the year, and family weekend activities enhance the museum experience.

KEEP IN MIND
The Burke has lots of special programs, mostly for older children and adults. Its weeklong summer camps inspire a love of science and history in kids ages 7–12. Lots of science-related events are held at the museum throughout the year, including Dinosaur Day, Native American Arts Celebration, and family weekend activities.

EATS FOR KIDS You can order sandwiches, salads, soups and pastries right at the museum, in the warm and inviting **Burke Café**. At **Atlas Foods** (2820 N.E. University Village Mall, tel. 206/522–6025), you can choose from such pan-American items as paella to grilled cheese, burgers, and noodles. **The Continental Restaurant & Pastry Shop** (4549 University Way N.E., tel. 206/632–4700) serves both Greek and American fare, plus breakfast all day.

CAMP 6 LOGGING MUSEUM

If you want to take your children back to an era when loggers hauled timber out of the woods to be loaded on steam trains, visit this museum where kids can see first-hand how lumbermen worked and lived.

Camp 6 was constructed using bits and pieces from logging camps all over the state. Period photos, equipment, and logging landscapes by a Northwest painter fill five red camp cars. Older children will enjoy these historical items, and younger ones will simply have fun running in and out of the "choo-choo" train. On the half-hour, an open-air, rough-and-ready utility logging train, built to haul boot-clad men takes you on a short ride. Little train buffs will get a kick out of watching a man jump off the train mid-trip to manually switch the tracks. Ask for a free railroad safety coloring book, and hang on tight to the kids.

As you bump along your way, the amiable "conductor" describes life at the camp. You'll pass an outdoor museum of logging equipment scattered through the woods, looking

KEEP IN MIND The museum is along a scenic 5-mile drive through regal forests and dramatic cliffsides, which lead down to the Puget Sound. After visiting the museum, you can hike or drive down to the beach.

HEY KIDS! Back in the 19th century, many workers rarely bathed. They believed it relaxed them and made them too weak to work. If you lived in a logging camp, you would be sharing a tiny train car with 40 other workers who hardly ever bathed. Maybe that bubble bath isn't such a bad thing after all!

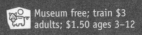
eerily ready for the workers to return from lunch. You can walk back later and take a closer look at the machinery, such as the 240-ton skidder, which was used to load timber onto log cars, and at the old "skid road," where logs were dragged downhill by a steam engine called a "donkey."

A hundred years ago, the loggers had their own version of the modern mobile home. They lived together in train cars, in logging camps like the one recreated here, where often as many as 40 lumbermen would bunk down in each cramped car. Your kids won't feel so bad about sharing their room after they take a look at these "bedrooms." Still, the men probably slept soundly after their grueling 16- to 18-hour days, six days a week—all for a buck a day!

EATS FOR KIDS Just a few blocks away, you'll find tasty, reasonably-priced Thai food at **Sar's** (4612 N. Pearl St., tel. 253/761–2727). You can order your noodles and soups mild for the little ones and spicy for grown-up tastes. If American is more your cuisine, grab a burger or sandwich at the **Shoboat Tavern** (5037 N. Pearl St., tel. 253/752–4128).

CARKEEK PARK

Tucked away in a tranquil north Seattle neighborhood, Carkeek Park is a hidden treasure of natural beauty. From its old-growth forest and salmon-spawning creek to sandy beach, it provides a dose of fresh air and fun for the whole family.

Entering through a deeply forested ridge that winds its way gracefully into the park, the whole family can explore trails leading through the woods and along Piper Creek. Some are flat enough for a stroller. A raised walkway leads from the forest to the beach side of the park, bridging the railroad tracks below. At low tide, kids can pick their way around the driftwood and poke about the tide pools for clams and mussels. Back on the forest side, the play area beckons the under-7 set with a stone salmon slide, an extra-long bouncing bridge, and assorted logs and rock "caves" for crawling.

At sunset, be sure you're facing west. As the sun melts into the Olympic Mountains,

KEEP IN MIND Wracking your brain for creative ideas for an upcoming birthday party? Let the naturalists at Carkeek give you a hand. You bring the cake and ice cream, and they'll tailor a program, complete with games and a nature walk to suit your child's interests. Spiders, squirrels, snakes, whatever—just let them know 3 weeks in advance. The kids will have a blast and take home something more lasting than party horns. The park can handle up to 20 children, ages 6 to 15. The cost is $90 for 10 kids; $120 for 20.

the entire park is bathed in shades of gold and pink. Kids get one of the best views of all, since the swings soar directly toward the Olympics.

The focus at Carkeek is on learning, and the Carkeek Park Environmental Education Center churns out terrific programs all year long, from guided bird and plant walks to bonfires and weeklong day camps. In winter, Carkeek livens up the cold months with Winter Voices, a program that brings in first-rate storytellers, singers, puppeteers, and naturalists to chase away those pre-spring blues.

Summer's arrival is celebrated with gusto. The annual festivities include a nature walk, bonfire, stories, and a drumming circle. Bring your own marshmallows, food, blankets, and a favorite musical instrument, and join the delightfully boisterous revelry.

GETTING THERE
You'll have to hunt for this gem. From I-5, turn west on N. Northgate Way, which becomes N. 105th St.; drive a mile, then turn right on Greenwood Ave. N. Go a half-mile and turn left on N.W. 110th St., which becomes Carkeek Park Road. The park entrance is on your left.

EATS FOR KIDS Picnic tables and grills are almost as abundant as natural beauty. Just pick your favorite view and spread your tablecloth. Extra-large sheltered grill areas keep the raindrops from dampening your fun. For an "indoor" feast, head to **Dick's Drive-In** (9208 Homan Rd. N.W., tel. 206/783-5233), a local landmark that serves terrific burgers, shakes, and lots of other goodies.

THE CENTER FOR WOODEN BOATS

It's not every museum that lets you walk all over the exhibits, then take them out for a spin. But that's exactly what the folks at this center want you to do. This mostly outdoor museum consists of docks lined with watercraft of all shapes, sizes, and ages that have been restored as good as new in the center's huge workshop. You're welcome to step inside any boat that suits your fancy, and most are available for rent.

Begin your trip by watching the volunteers patch up the vintage vessels in the workshop. The eager staff will tell you about the boats, their history, and what it takes to get them back in ship-shape. Kids can check out their muscle power at an exhibit that shows how a pulley is used to lift a load onto a boat. As you step inside the center's main building, the Boathouse, tell the kids to look up. Hanging from the ceiling is a 12-foot Eskimo kayak and a half-dozen other historic boats. Informative signs explain how each type of vessel was used.

KEEP IN MIND The 165-foot-long *Wawona*, docked just beside the museum, gives kids a rare chance to see what life was like aboard a schooner during the turn of the 20th century. You can explore this aging beauty's decks, galley, cabins, and cargo hold for free.

HEY KIDS! Nowadays, when we think of boats, we usually think of fun—lazy days out on the lake, fishing for dinner on a camping trip, or maybe even taking a cruise to somewhere exotic. But at one time, crews lived and worked on boats for months at a time, especially during fishing season. On a sailing schooner like the *Wawona*, 30 men would share one room full of bunks for half the year. Even if they loved the sea, you can bet they were happy to get back home!

1010 Valley St.

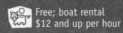 Free; boat rental $12 and up per hour

May-Sep, daily 11–7; Oct–Feb, W–Su 11–5; Mar–Apr, W–Su 11–6

206/382–2628; www.cwb.org

5 and up

After seeing the museum sights, you can then pick out a historic boat for an hour of rowing—or sailing—around Lake Union; life jackets are provided. Budding sailors can take individual lessons for $30 an hour.

A much pricier, but certainly unforgettable, summertime experience is the center's Adventure Bound program, for kids ages 14–18. Youngsters live on a 100-foot schooner for a week and sail around the San Juan Islands. No experience is necessary, and the $575 tuition includes food and lodging. But the best bargain at the center can be found every Sunday, at 2 PM, when you can get a free ride on a classic sailboat, weather permitting. Happy sails!

EATS FOR KIDS Just north of the Center for Wooden Boats, you'll find several restaurants clustered along South Lake Union. At **Duke's Lake Union Chowderhouse** (901 Fairview N., tel. 206/382–9963) the seafood dishes may be a bit steep, but the children's menu is $5 per meal. On a sunny day, you can sit outside and watch the seaplanes take off and land. **Chandler's Crabhouse & Fresh Fish Market** (901 Fairview N., tel. 206/223–2722), a local favorite, serves seafood.

THE CHILDREN'S MUSEUM

At last, a museum with the youngest children in mind! At this playtime paradise underneath the Seattle Center, kids will learn plenty as they discover the myriad displays.

Exhibits are divided into various action-packed "adventures." For kids up to age 2, the watery world of Discovery Bay is the main attraction, with its colorful fish darting through a huge aquarium along one wall. Toddlers will head straight for the "ferry boat" slide and giant busyboard. When they're done, books and toys scattered about the floor and tables await. At Mountain Forest, kids can slide on a glacier, crawl in hollow logs, and explore a hillside. Remind them to check under the rocks, where lots of animals are hiding. Even in this childhood fantasy world, the talking trees may surprise the grown-ups!

At the Global Village, kids get the flavor of faraway lands. They can hop on a bus or ship, train or tricycle, and visit places such as Ghana and Japan. It's a great multicultural experience, with something fun to do—from shopping in the market to playing the drums—at each stop.

HEY KIDS! When you visit the Global Village, you'll notice that things are different from your hometown. That's because people around the world have different ways of dressing, foods to eat, and houses. But not everything is different. No matter where you go, kids love to play, sing, and spend time with their families, just like you!

 305 Harrison St.

 $5 ages 1 and up

M–F 10–5, Sa–Su 10–6

206/441–1768;
www.thechildrensmuseum.org

1–10

If you have a budding artist, don't miss the Artists' Studio, where kids work alongside a real artist-in-residence. Smocks and supplies are provided, and the artist will happily offer pointers. For budding builders, a room with Legos, Lincoln Logs, and boxes of assorted sizes for stacking will surely engage. In the summertime, kids can "ooh" and "ahh" over elaborate sand castles built by local crafters, then dig into the sandboxes and create their own.

The Center hosts a variety of special programs including Storytelling Circle, where talented storytellers read popular children's books. At the Evening Arts Camp, children are introduced to art through games, stories, and videos.

No matter what your kids' interests are, a world of discovery awaits; a good imagination is the only passport needed.

EATS FOR KIDS
Upstairs at the Center House, try **Quincy's Center House Restaurant** (tel. 206/728–2228) for tasty children's fare or **Steamers** (tel. 206/728–2228) for seafood-lovers. Both are reasonably priced.

KEEP IN MIND Your children will do a lot of crawling, climbing, and painting, so leave the good clothes at home. Rugged, washable clothing and rubber-soled shoes are recommended.

COUGAR MOUNTAIN ZOOLOGICAL PARK

59

When you take a walk on the wild side at this zoo, you'll notice something special about the animals—they're among the last of their kind on Earth. This unique zoo takes in and breeds rare and endangered mammals and birds.

Your park experience begins with a burst of outrageous colors from the macaws and parrots. These feathered mimics delight children by calling out cheerful greetings, except for one naughty parrot, who wolf-whistles and cries "Woo!" Quieter but more whimsical are the larger birds. The East African Crowned Crane always turns heads with its spiky hairdo, and so does the red-headed Sarus Crane.

Toward the back of the park, sleek cougars prowl their surroundings, safely separated from animals such as the Lowland Nyala antelopes. Leave plenty of time for the lively lemurs, whose antics will inspire giggles even in a 2-year-old (and their screeching will make your 2-year-old seem serene). At Santa's Reindeer Farm, Siberian reindeer munch

KEEP IN MIND Since this park is so compact, let your novice walker toddle around without bringing a stroller. And if walking past the habitats doesn't burn off enough energy, the grassy areas where you can turn them loose surely will.

HEY KIDS! The large gray birds with the red heads are called Sarus Cranes. They live in Asia and Australia, and in some ways, they're a lot like people. They can get up to 7 feet tall, making them the tallest flying bird in the world. They can even live up to 70 or 80 years. They also mate for life; the mother and father build their nest together and raise one baby at a time.

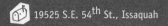 19525 S.E. 54th St., Issaquah

 $8 adults,
$5.50 ages 4–15,
$4 ages 2–3

Mar–Oct, F–Su 10–5 (Reindeer Festival in December)

1 and up

425/391–5508

contentedly on the hillside. If you go in the springtime, the kids can see baby deer following their mothers around. For $1, kids can buy a cup of fruit to hand-feed the deerlike Formosa Sika, which are extinct in the wild, and the red alpacas, with their comical red mops of hair and big, crooked teeth.

In December, Cougar Mountain holds its popular Reindeer Festival, with Santa greeting children from his fancy sleigh, elves telling stories, and the grounds festively adorned. Free special presentations are held throughout the festival and feature various animals. Watch Comet the reindeer strut around and display his antlers; kids can even come up to pet him. They can also watch cougars as they hunt in the yard for treats hidden there by the staff. These up-close animal interactions are terrific for kids ages 2 and up.

EATS FOR KIDS There are no restaurants in the immediate area, but you can picnic on the large patio with tables and a scenic view of Lake Sammamish and the Cascade Mountains. You can buy soft drinks from the vending machine.

DISCOVERY PARK

This park truly lives up to its name. You never know when you'll see a bald eagle soaring above the trees, a salamander sliding through a pond, or a crab scampering along the shore. Even an old lighthouse, a hilltop full of historic Army buildings, and a spectacular Native American mural await discovery.

A number of trails traverse the park. The 2.8-mile Loop Trail circles through a diverse landscape: deep forest, sandy and rocky beaches, dramatic cliffsides, pungent wetlands, and grassy green meadows. The more family-friendly quarter-mile Wolf Trail crosses a babbling creek on its way through an area that was logged in the late 1800s but is now filled with native plants. Pushing a stroller along the uneven path is tricky, so a baby backpack might be a better idea. You can also stick to one of the many paved trails.

Discovery Park was once a sprawling military compound called Fort Lawton. Nearly all of the base's 500-plus acres are now a natural sanctuary for birds and wildlife. As you wander

HEY KIDS! You might be surprised to learn that park rangers and community volunteers are working hard to get rid of some of the plants at Discovery Park. Why on earth would they want to do that? Over the years, plants brought from many other parts of the world into Puget Sound have begun to push out the native vegetation that once thrived here. To preserve the native plants and trees, workers are yanking out such plants as English Ivy, Scot's broom, and Himalayan blackberry.

around the park, traces of its previous Army base life peek out. The historic officers' quarters are still inhabited by military personnel.

Another inhabitant of this park is the Daybreak Star Center. It was built after Native Americans occupied the area for three months in 1970, demanding the entire locale be turned over to them instead of converted into a public park. Daybreak Star was a concession. In addition to childcare, educational, and elder-care services, this facility houses a large permanent collection of traditional and contemporary Native American art and colorful murals.

With its wildlife and plants in the forest, this park provides an exciting, tangible outdoor classroom for kids to enjoy and learn about nature.

KEEP IN MIND
On Saturdays at 2 PM, a naturalist leads a free nature walk. You need to call the visitor center by 8:30 AM to sign up. Whatever day you come, make the most of your visit by stopping by the center for a map of the park.

EATS FOR KIDS Discovery Park is one of Seattle's most popular picnic spots; just pick your view and claim your table. If you'd rather dine out, try the terrific seafood and sandwiches at **Chinook's at Salmon Bay** (1900 W. Nickerson St., tel. 206/283-4665), a lively, local favorite down the road at the Fisherman's Terminal.

EVERGREEN ALPACA FARM

57

What's that curious creature poking its tousled mop at you, bad dental work in full view? Say hello to an alpaca. These congenial, South American animals closely resemble their larger llama cousins. But the ones roaming around this farm are not just your run-of-the-mill alpacas. Evergreen owner Lorie Hull has had winners in the Alpacapalooza competition for three years running. Yes, there is such a thing as an alpaca show.

Lorie cares for more than a dozen of these amusing creatures. During spring to fall, you'll even see two or three babies, called crias, toddling around. Children of all ages delight in petting and feeding these odd but sweet-faced creatures, which are about the size of big dogs. All the alpacas are tame, and the adult animals seem to have a special fondness for human "crias," especially if their fists are stuffed with tender grain. But younger

EATS FOR KIDS Gig Harbor has lots of interesting shops and restaurants. **Spiro's** (3108 Harborview Dr., tel. 253/851-9200) serves tasty Italian food at reasonable prices. For Mexican, drive uphill from the waterfront to fun, friendly **Moctezumas** (4803 Pt. Fosdick Dr., tel. 253/851-8464).

GETTING THERE Take I–5 south to the Gig Harbor/Bremerton exit, then cross the Tacoma Narrows Bridge (Highway 16) and take the City Center exit. Turn left on Wollochet, right at the light onto Hunt, then right on 46th. Next take a left on Rosedale, right on 86th, and right on David Day. Take the right before a group of four mailboxes—2 black, 1 green, 1 white—then stay to the left and watch for sign for Evergreen's driveway.

8815 82nd Avenue N.W., Gig Harbor

Free

Call ahead

253/851–5538;
www.alpacawa.org

2 and up

tots who might be a bit intimidated by even the gentlest hairy beast can always throw a ball for Lorie's black lab, Holly, instead.

In addition to Lorie's prized herd, you might spot a few other wild critters frolicking around the farm. While you're communing with the alpacas, keep your eyes peeled for Canadian geese, coyotes, pheasants, ducks, deer, and a dozen kinds of songbirds. Evergreen is a mini-wildlife preserve of sorts.

And don't forget your camera—those pictures of the kids nuzzling a few shaggy heads, grins all around, are priceless.

KEEP IN MIND For a picnic or a little playful respite, stop by the Kopachuck State Park near Gig Harbor. (You will have passed the turnoff on Rosedale). Open year-round from dawn till dusk, this tucked-away gem has sandy beaches, hiking, unbeatable sunsets, and an incredible panorama of the Olympics and Puget Sound. You'll find dozens of picnic tables and four kitchen shelters with electricity.

EXPERIENCE MUSIC PROJECT

If someone in your family wants to become a rock star, here's their big chance! At this one-of-a-kind music museum, the whole family can get into the act. The focus here is to inspire a love of music through an array of creative, hands-on exhibits. Rock, blues, jazz, punk, soul and country—they all share the same high-tech spotlight.

The EMP's Sound Lab is decked out with the latest in high-tech audio equipment and computer graphics. Kids can grab a guitar, bass, keyboard or drum for a live performance in front of a "virtual" audience of screaming fans. Beginners can program their instruments to show them the right notes to play, and proficient musicians can opt to do it themselves. With this set-up, even a family of novices can come up with a pretty impressive "Louie Louie." When your group has finished jamming, you can buy a poster of your family "band." In the process, kids will learn how music is made.

HEY KIDS! If the Experience Music Project building looks like a huge piece of twisted metal to you, you're not alone. But if you were flying overhead in an airplane, it would look just like a smashed guitar. That's because it was modeled after a famous guitar that rock guitarist Jimi Hendrix smashed during a London concert in 1967. See if you can find the snapped "strings" on the roof.

325 5th Ave. N.

 $20 adult, $16 ages
13–17, $15 ages 7–12

Su–Th 9–9, F–Sa 9 AM–11 PM

877/367–5483;
www.emplive.com

7 and up

The historic exhibits will have limited appeal to pre-teens, but teenagers may appreciate that punk and grunge are included in the mix. Mom and Dad, however, may be the only ones reminiscing over memorabilia from such groups as Heart and Queensrÿche—or over the Hendrix Gallery, the core of this museum, which was built as a tribute to the late guitarist Jimi Hendrix. Nevertheless, kids may at least pick up on the contribution of early rock to the music they enjoy today. As long as your kids are over 7, the EMP is bound to strike the right chord.

Be sure to visit the EMP store. You and the kids can listen to your hearts' content to an incredible variety of music. The CDs are for sale, but you can listen for free. Make your selections on the computer, put on the headphones, and enjoy!

KEEP IN MIND
This area around the EMP is perfectly safe in the daytime, but walking around here at night is not recommended.

EATS FOR KIDS **The Turntable Restaurant** (tel. 206/770–2777) inside the EMP is a lively, colorful spot to dine, and a favorite with kids. The children's menu, priced at $5 per meal, includes fun items such as "Gobs O' Noodles." Adults can order anything from a salad to a fine seafood entrée. You can also walk a couple of blocks over to **Zeek's** (419 Denny Way, tel. 206/448–6775), one of the best pizza places in Seattle. It's more funky than pretty, but the service and food are great.

FORT NISQUALLY

Travel back in time at this living history museum, where volunteers and staff, in period clothing, engage visitors with 19th century craft demonstrations and entertain with period music and dialogue. Its huge, grassy clearing framed by Douglas firs evokes the frontier spirit of the times—and also provides kids with lots of room to stretch out.

In the mid-1800s, the Hudson Bay Company of London owned this bustling fur-trading outpost. Local Indian tribes brought endless stacks of pelts—beaver, otter, fox, muskrat, rabbit—to be pressed into huge bales and shipped to Europe and China, where they were made into hats and clothing. Encourage children to imagine life at the outpost as you poke around the kitchen, lookout towers, blacksmith shop, and trading store. Most of the buildings were recreated, but two—the officer's house and the granary—are historic landmarks, moved from their original location 17 miles south.

GETTING THERE Drive south on I-5 to Exit 132, then take Highway 16 to 6th Avenue. Turn left on 6th Street, then turn right onto Pearl Street and follow the signs to Point Defiance. Signs will lead you to Fort Nisqually.

EATS FOR KIDS If you have giant-slayers or pumpkin-eaters in your family, bring a sack lunch to nibble at **Never Never Land,** a free park next door to Fort Nisqually. Packed with playhouses, nature trails, and nursery-rhyme statues, it's a lunchtime adventureland. Picnic tables are tucked away among the scenic winding trails, and a large grouping of tables, beside a playhouse, can be reserved for birthday parties. A small playground provides a spot for after-lunch antics.

5400 N. Pearl St. #11, Tacoma

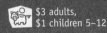 $3 adults,
$1 children 5–12

 Apr–Sep daily, Oct–Mar W–Su;
opens 11 AM, closing times vary

253/591–5339;
www.fortnisqually.org

6 and up

The trading store's shelves are piled with merchandise favored by local Indians, such as wool blankets, ivory combs, women's stockings and flour. A glimpse into the workers' quarters will give kids a taste of daily life at the fort. Ten to 20 men usually lived on the grounds, along with their children and wives, in cramped, cozy living spaces, where beds, table, cookstove, cradle, washstand, and chamber pot were all crammed together.

Outside, Fort Nisqually kids had room to play and lots of homemade toys to amuse themselves. Staff members demonstrate a few of these primitive amusements, and your kids can try them out. You can even buy the toys in the museum gift shop and take home a bit of 19th century life.

HEY KIDS! If you lived at Fort Nisqually in 1833, you'd have lots of work to do, helping out with such chores as gardening and fetching water from the well. For fun, you'd roam in meadows and play with wooden toys. You'd probably play a game called Graces, in which each player held a stick and tossed wooden hoops back and forth.

FUNTASIA

"You must have fun" is the rule here. It's a rule that's hard to break, whether you're a jubilant kid climbing, tunneling, sliding and bouncing through 4,000 square feet of fun or an adult chuckling over your child's antics.

The Fun Fortress section mostly appeals to kids under 6. In the ball pit area, even toddlers can jump and wade through the hundreds of colorful plastic balls and "bury" each other for fun. Kids no taller than 4' 8" are challenged by a tricky obstacle course that involves scaling a steep mat on a rope. Children must be supervised in the Fun Fortress area.

For kids who have moved beyond the ball-pit stage, seven more acres of entertainment await their more sophisticated tastes. In the video arcade, the neon lights flash continuously—and so do the eyes of kids as they gleefully slam levers. The selection

EATS FOR KIDS You can recharge your little adventurers' batteries without ever leaving the premises. Funtasia's **café** serves hot dogs, pizza, chicken nuggets, among other goodies, from $1.50 and up. A mile down Aurora Avenue, you can dine at the **Family Pancake House** (23725 Hwy 99, tel. 425/775–6300) in Edmonds. You'll find everything from Crepes Suzette to oysters; a child's stack of three generous-sized pancakes costs about a buck.

7212 220th St. SW, Edmonds (I-5 north
to 220th St. exit, head west one mile)

 Activities priced
separately, discount
passes available

 Su–Th 10–10; F–Sa 10 AM–12 AM

425/774-4263

1 and up

of games appeals both to girls and boys, ages 5 and up. Some games can handle up to six players, so a whole group can join in. To keep Mom and Dad amused, Funtasia has dusted off a few oldie-goldies—Ms. PacMan, Asteroids, and air hockey.

Older kids can try their hand at Lazer Tag or ride on the GoKarts or the outdoor Bumper Boats. The whole family can play indoor putt-putt, a perfect activity for rainy days. Even tots get to choose their own small plastic clubs and "play" along. For the heavy-hitters in your family, the batting cages have 12 hardball and softball pitching machines.

If your kids deserve a treat—or if you just want a good night's sleep—this spot will bring smiles and burn off energy. Funtasia is 15 miles north of Seattle.

KEEP IN MIND
This popular spot can get swamped with kids on the weekend, so take advantage of the weekday evening hours to avoid the crowds. To make sure you'll have plenty of elbow room, go before or after dinner.

HEY, KIDS! Got a younger brother or sister who's always pestering you to include them in your fun? You might score some brownie points with your sibling—and make their day—by inviting he or she to share your GoKart or Bumper Boat ride. Very young children may be too short to go on these rides by themselves, but with you along, they might just stack up!

GAMEWORKS

Forget the days of standing for hours in front of a pinball machine. Nothing stands still for long in this virtual-reality fantasyland. Kids can grab a pair of oars and guide a careening kayak downriver, slip into a pair of waterskis and try to stay afloat, slip a fire-hose strap over their shoulders and douse a blistering blaze, or hop on a motorcycle and rev it up for a race. Almost any outdoor adventure a kid could imagine is available here in high-motion, electronic form.

Many of the games are competitions, and it's more fun for youngsters if they bring their "opponents" along with them. At the Indy 500, a real person announces the race as up to eight contestants steer full-size NASCAR replicas along a virtual track. For the brave, the Vertical Reality games raise the level of excitement even higher. In one of them, Sky Pirates, players sit in mechanical cars that leap 24 feet into the air, where they drop virtual hot-air balloons—armed with weapons—onto opponents' balloons.

HEY KIDS!

Don't worry about lugging around a pock-etful of change or to-kens at GameWorks. You buy cards with set amounts of money, then pop them into each game before you play. The card automatically subtracts until it's used up.

EATS FOR KIDS The **GameWorks Grill** is a full-service restaurant, serving a range of items from chicken wings to steaks at reasonable prices. But if you need a break from the sensory overload, walk across to **The Cheesecake Factory** (700 Pike St., tel. 206/652–5400), where a huge menu lists a plethora of choices from bite-size burgers to filet mignon.

1511 7th Ave.

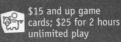 $15 and up game cards; $25 for 2 hours unlimited play

M–Th 11 AM–12 AM, F 11 AM–1 AM, Sa 10 AM–1 AM, Su 10 AM–12 AM

206/521–0950; www.gameworks.com

 7 and up

There are a number of weapon-toting games, but one of the most popular games is completely non-violent. In Dance Dance Revolution, players pick a popular song, then step on lighted arrows in sequence with arrows that appear on the screen. If you want to see some really fancy footwork, stand near this game and wait for a good contestant to show up. You'll be astounded.

You'll also find a few retro games, such as air hockey, PacMan, and Asteroids, lurking about. Upstairs, the Big Win Zone is filled with such games as Skee Ball and mechanical "grabbers," which spit out tickets that can be accumulated and redeemed for prizes. Be prepared, though—it can be pretty loud.

If you're looking for an educational family outing, this probably isn't it. But if you want to give the kids a thrill, there's virtually no better place to go.

KEEP IN MIND All the games have signs informing parents of their suitability for various ages and warning of any violent content, whether mild or strong, lifelike or animated. These labels are quite helpful, and parents are advised to read them. Children under 16 should not be left alone to make their own selections without adult supervision.

GAS WORKS PARK

I f all you see are rusty old pipes when you arrive at this park, don't worry—you're in the right place! Seattlelites like to recycle everything, and that goes for playground equipment, too. Just follow one of the dirt trails over the knoll and you'll see that this is definitely a place for kids.

What was once an old gas-manufacturing plant from 1906 has been transformed into one of the city's best recreation areas. As you wander around its 20 acres, expect a few surprises. The old boiler house is now a picnic shelter with grills and tables, and the exhauster-compressor building now houses a children's play barn, with splashes of brightly colored paint making the long-retired equipment seem almost whimsical.

Outside the barn, the playground blends modern equipment with climbable relics. Down at the lakefront, you can picnic, sun, or watch boats sail dreamily by on Lake Union. Most

GETTING THERE Gas Works Park can be a bit tricky to find. From I–5, take the Mercer Street exit onto Fairview, bear right toward Seattle Center, then turn left onto Valley. Stay in the right lane and curve right at the bend onto Westlake Avenue. Bear right and follow Westlake across the Fremont Bridge, then take an immediate right onto North-lake. You'll see a sign and large parking area on the right.

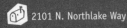

kids, however, will insist on climbing the tall hill. Once they reach the top, they'll discover a breathtaking view of the city across Lake Union and a large sundial.

On the other side of the hill, kites of all shapes and sizes are usually sailing in the breeze. Be sure to bring one along; this classic amusement never fails to captivate kids. Another big attraction for youngsters is rolling down the soft green hillsides. With slopes of varying slants, taking a tumble is great fun for most any age child. Outside the park, skaters zip along the sidewalk that winds around the lakefront. Bring along your skates and the whole family can take a tour on wheels.

HEY KIDS! Sundials have been keeping track of time for thousands of years. Long before clocks were invented, someone noticed that a pointer aimed at the celestial pole would cast a shadow in the same location on a circle every day. Voila! People could start getting to their appointments on time.

EATS FOR KIDS You can grab a sandwich at **Stoneway Café** (3620 Stone Way N., tel. 206/547-9958) to stay or to go and gobble them at the park. For burgers or gyros, try **Costa Opa** (3400 Fremont Ave. N., tel. 206/633-4141). Although it lacks a children's menu, the folks here are happy to prepare a grilled cheese sandwich or linguine with parmesan. Everyone can enjoy the mouthwatering baklava for dessert.

GREEN LAKE PARK

This charming oasis in the middle of an urban neighborhood north of downtown is spacious, lovingly tended, and draped around a picturesque lake. Walkers, joggers, skaters, bicycles, and every kind of dog imaginable happily share the scenery along its 2.8-mile path.

The playground is among the city's most creative, and it's wisely divided into sections for younger children and grade-schoolers. At the large sandy area, your child can hop on a crane, complete with levers to work the shovel. You'll often find a line of eager 4- to 7-year-old boys waiting their turn to dig in. Bring buckets and shovels to keep your little diggers occupied while they wait for the coveted crane.

Other amusements include colorful giant spinners, wheels and levers, lots of climbing equipment, a spin-around, swings, and slides. Be sure to bring the bathing suits so

HEY KIDS!

Beautiful Green Lake is 50,000 years old. It may look calm today, but it's seen plenty of action. A massive glacier moving along the land formed the lake, which contains ash from a volcano that erupted in the area about 7,000 years ago.

EATS FOR KIDS You'll find plenty of restaurants and shops directly across the street from the park. **Spud Fish & Chips** (6860 E. Green Lake Way N., tel. 206/524–0565) is popular with the kids, or try **Tacos Guaymas** (6808 E. Green Lake Way N., tel. 206/729–6563) for authentic Mexican food. If you just have the munchies, the **snack stand** at the park sells pretzels, cookies, and drinks.

 7201 East Green Lake Drive N.

 Free; pool session
$1.75 children
$2.50 adults

 Park daily; pool M–Sa, wading
pool/boat rental summertime

206/684–4075, 206/684–4961 pool;
206/684–7796 wading pool

All ages

everyone can take a dip. In the summertime, lifeguards are on duty at the swimming beaches. But before you jump in the lake, check for signs warning of algae blooms, a common problem on warm days. You can enjoy Green Lake's six-lane indoor pool any time of year. In the summer months, the little ones can chill out in the outdoor wading pool. You can also rent a canoe or a paddle boat, or try your hand at fishing.

Green Lake is also a site for a variety of events and festivities. In July, the Milk Carton Derby pits amazingly creative boats made of—you guessed it—milk cartons against each other for prizes. So drink up!

KEEP IN MIND The path around the lake is divided into two lanes: fast and slow. Bikers and skateboarders get to zip along in the fast lane; while the slower one is reserved for strollers, walkers, joggers, and children who are a bit unsteady on their skates or tricycles.

HIRAM CHITTENDON LOCKS

eaping lizards! No, wait, they're salmon, bounding their way up the Lake Washington Ship Canal Fish Ladder on their trek back from the Pacific Ocean to the streams where they were born. How do they know where to go? Nobody knows. But they'll do whatever it takes to get there, so they can spawn another generation in the exact location where they started out. To a salmon, there's no place like home.

The salmon put on a fascinating show for the million or so annual visitors to Hiram Chittendon Locks, the gateway from the ocean and Puget Sound to Lake Washington and the salmon streams. You can see all kinds of salmon swimming through the locks all year long, but the sockeye run—from July through September—is the biggest and best. Even babies love to watch the silvery fish leap up the 21-step ladder. For toddlers and older kids, a lesson in persistence is to be learned; it may take a fish several tries to make it up each step. You can watch the performance from outdoor overlooks or a large underwater-viewing area with lighted windows.

HEY KIDS! While adult salmon "climb" the ladder to swim upstream, tiny salmon called smolts swim downstream, on their way out to sea. But diving off the dam is dangerous for the smolts, so the Corps of Engineers installed watery chutes to help them take the plunge safely. As you walk across the bridge to the fish ladder, you can see these chutes—which are full of fish so small you may not be able to see them—pour out of large white pipes.

 3015 NW 54th St.

206/783-7059

Free

Daily 7 AM-9 PM

All ages

As mesmerizing as it is to watch the high-hurdling fish, leave time to enjoy the rest of the park. The locks are educational and fun; you can cross the footbridge to watch them. You'll see boats of all shapes and sizes traveling between the Sound and the lake, ranging from fishing boats to sightseeing vessels to huge container ships en route to Alaska. Boaters waiting for the water to rise wave up at the kids lining the railings. By the time the locks are opened, children are delighted to discover that the vessels are nearly eye-level.

On your way in or out, stop by the visitor center, which has a bookstore and exhibits about salmon and the locks sure to pique the interest of children 7 and up. If you'd like a free guided tour by a U.S. Corps of Engineers ranger, you can sign up here.

EATS FOR KIDS
Just outside the locks entrance, the **Lockspot Café** (3005 N.W. 54th St., 206/789-4865) serves up scrumptious fish 'n' chips, burgers, and other lunchtime goodies. If your mood is more south-of-the-border, try **Taco Time** (2853 N.W. Market, tel. 206/789-2344) across the street.

KEEP IN MIND After you've visited the locks and fish ladder, take some time to smell the flowers. The beautifully landscaped grounds around the locks include a splendid botanical garden that is usually bursting with color and fragrance. It was built by a Corpsman who decided to create a little paradise out of the land left empty after the locks were completed in 1917.

HURRICANE RIDGE

Amid the stunning Olympic National Park, Hurricane Ridge puts you at eye level with the tip-tops of the surrounding majestic peaks. On a clear day, you can see Mount Olympus and Canada. This is the 5,000-foot-high view of a lifetime.

In the summertime, the meadows burst with outrageous wildflowers, the black-tailed deer wander around hoping for hand-outs, and the alpine trails beckon visitors to check out just one more glorious vista. In the wintertime, the scenery is just as spectacular; snowshoe tours and skiing are particularly inviting. Hurricane Ridge is also known for its sudden storms; always call the recorded hotline before you go.

Late spring through fall is the best time for traveling to Hurricane Ridge with children. You'll find enticing trails at every level of difficulty. If you're pushing a stroller or have a little one toddling along, stick with the short, paved Meadow Loop Trails, which begin at the visitor center. With older children, head to Hurricane Hill, a scenic 3-mile loop

EATS FOR KIDS Pack a picnic and pick a spot on the alpine meadow, where the drama includes wildlife and heart-stopping scenery. In nearby Port Angeles, pick one of its fine cafes along the waterfront. At **First Street Haven** (107 E. 1st St., tel. 360/457–0352) locals swear by the chili and sandwiches.

HEY KIDS! Hurricane Ridge is part of the Olympic Mountains, on the Olympic Peninsula, which juts out toward Canada. On the west side of the peninsula is the Pacific Ocean; on the east is the Puget Sound. Across Puget Sound lies Seattle, which is smack dab in the middle of two mountain ranges. The Olympics tower to the west and the Cascades, which include the famous Mount Rainier, rise to the east.

3002 Mount Angeles Rd.,
17 miles south of Port Angeles

 360/565-3130 visitor center; 360/565-3131
weather and road conditions recording

 $10 to drive
up Hurricane
Ridge Road

Road open Fr–Su in winter, daily spring
through fall; call ahead for road condition
and visitor center hours

All ages

that starts at the end of Hurricane Ridge Road. The uphill climb is moderate, and the payoff—
a view from a former lookout on the very top—is unbeatable. This hike takes three or four
hours with kids along.

The visitor center is staffed in hiking season, and has clean restrooms and exhibits on the
national park's ecology, native plants, and animals. If you want to stay longer than a day,
you can camp in one of many designated campgrounds or stay at a motel in nearby Port
Angeles. Even if you don't stay overnight, consider a stop in town anyway. The waterfront,
just a ferry ride away from Victoria, Canada, is fun to explore. There's a tall observation
tower, in case you didn't get enough scenery on Hurricane Ridge, and an aquatic center
where kids can bond with dozens of sea creatures.

With its lush rain forest and ancient trees—some believed to be 1,000 years old—
Hurricane Ridge is truly a mountaintop experience!

GETTING THERE Take the Bainbridge Island ferry, then
head north on S.R. 305 and follow the signs to the Hood Canal. Cross the
bridge and follow S.R. 104 onto U.S. Highway 101 toward Port Angeles. Once
in town, turn left on Race Street, and follow it into Olympic National Park.
Hurricane Ridge is about 80 miles from Seattle.

INTERNATIONAL DISTRICT

Meander though the International District for a concentrated taste of a diverse blend of Asian cultures. The colors, smells, and tastes are intoxicating to young and old alike.

The first Asians to arrive in Seattle were Chinese, mostly single men who came seeking their fortune in the new boomtown starting in the 1860s. They worked in the restaurants, canneries, shops, and hotels, banding together near the train station and waterfront. Then came Japanese in the 1890s, settling just north of Chinatown, who opened laundries, markets, and restaurants. The third Asian group, Filipinos, became a presence in Seattle in the early 1900s, working in hotels and running pool halls and barbershops. In the 1980s, Vietnamese refugees poured into the area, opening clothing stores, markets, and restaurants.

Pick up your map for a self-guided tour of the district from the Wing Luke Asian Museum (*see* #2). The walk is a few blocks for the main sights and even easier if you work in a few breaks for tasty treats. Tour highlights include the Tsue Chong Noodle Company (801–811

HEY KIDS! The goodies you see in Chinese bakeries may not look like the cakes and cookies you're used to eating. But give them a try and you'll find out they're just as delicious. Just remember, to girls and boys in China your yummy chocolate-chip cookies might seem just as strange as those pineapple buns seem to you!

S. King St.), a fourth-generation business that makes more than a dozen kinds of Chinese noodles and fortune cookies. Another is Uwajimaya (519 6th Ave. S.), a Japanese supermarket and bookstore with a dazzling array of Asian produce and imports. Run by the son of a Japanese immigrant who started the business as a small fish market, it's about as close as you can get to Japan on this side of the ocean. The Vietnamese Viet Wah Supermarket (1035 S. Jackson St.) entices visitors with its exotic fruits and vegetables, colorful displays, and bustling crowds speaking a variety of languages.

As you wander, you'll be tempted to pop inside a dozen shops full of trinkets, fish and sundries—such as the Higo Variety Store (602–608 S. Jackson St.), one of the last Japanese-American businesses left from before World War II. Don't resist the temptation!

EATS FOR KIDS

Many of the restaurants here serve dim sum (Chinese hors d'oeuvres) for lunch; but stick with noodles for the little ones. Excellent choices include the **China Gate Restaurant** (514–518 7th Ave. S., tel. 206/624–1730) and **Sun-Ya** (605 7th Ave. S., tel. 206/623–1670). For Asian pastries and cakes, try **Sun Bakery** (at 658 S. Jackson St., tel. 206/622–9288).

KEEP IN MIND For an escorted tour of the International District, call Vi Mar at Chinatown Discovery (tel. 425/885-3085). She conducts a variety of tours, with and without meals. For example, "Nibble Your Way Through Chinatown" lets you graze at several spots. Family tour prices start at about $23 per adult and $8 for children ages 5–11. Vi knows the district inside and out, and she's good with kids.

KLONDIKE GOLD RUSH MUSEUM

Gold fever! You can feel it in the air at this memorial to the thousands of "stampeders" who braved the elements to seek their fortunes in the Yukon more than a century ago.

Through displays, the era comes alive for kids, especially if you've briefed them on the story of the Gold Rush before your visit. They'll discover that a lot of kids went along on the adventure as they look at the pictures of stampeder families. A variety of items such as a camp stove, compasses, and footwear demonstrate how these families lived their lives. Help your kids imagine the well-worn boots trudging through the snowy mountains on exhausted but hopeful miner's feet.

Appropriately tucked away in historic Pioneer Square, the museum shows films in its auditorium throughout the day, with period photography, music, and readings from

KEEP IN MIND The gift shop sells a variety of inexpensive souvenirs to help kids remember their history lesson. Those old enough to enjoy the exhibits can buy their own gold nugget for just $3 or a book about families who traveled to the Yukon. Even the youngest tots will have fun with a Gold Rush coloring book.

HEY KIDS! For prospectors, getting to the gold fields was hard but looking for gold once you got there was easy. Since it's one of the heaviest metals, gold sinks to the bottom of the stream—and the bottom of a pan. Miners dipped their pans in the water, then looked for gold on the bottom. But although looking for gold was easy, actually finding it was another matter. Of the thousands of people who went in search of gold, few ever found any!

 117 S. Main Street

 Free

Daily 9–5

 206/553-7220

7 and up

stampeders' journals. You can almost feel the weight of the pickax and the bite of the wind. The films also show how the trails look today, with remnants of long-gone miners left along the way, in memory of those who got rich—and the thousands who didn't. Some children may get fidgety when the still photos are shown, but the films last less than a half hour, so most kids do just fine. If you have restless kids, sit near the back for an easy exit.

In the summertime, park rangers from the museum present a variety of programs, including free tours of the historic Pioneer Square area, Seattle's original settlement. Many historic buildings remain from the late 1890s, including the Globe Hotel, which now houses the well-known Elliott Bay Bookstore. You'll also see the remnants of Cooper & Levy, a major outfitting store for the prospectors. Happy digging!

EATS FOR KIDS **Quizno's Subs** (221 1st St., tel. 206/621–7787) serves up a variety of fresh sandwiches for a quick lunch. On those chilly Seattle days, chase away the shivers with a warm bowl of soup at **Soup Daddy Soups** (106 Occidental St., tel. 206/682–7202). Favorites include chicken chili, garden vegetable, and Popeye's Special, a cream of mushroom soup with spinach. Soup Daddy also serves salads, chicken, and other items.

LAKE FOREST PARK

G ot youngsters of assorted ages and tastes? This one-stop entertainment shop is just the ticket to make everybody happy. Its variety of climbing, jumping, spinning, tunneling and digging equipment is truly amazing. The hanging and climbing bars are challenging enough to keep older kids happy while their younger siblings frolic. Your neighborhood playground will never look the same again!

But wait, there's more. If you have trouble dragging the kids away from the playground, just utter the magic word "pony"! On summer weekends from 2 to 3 PM, kids 2 and older (and weighing less than 70 pounds) can take a free pony ride. Mom or Dad can hang onto tots during the ride. Downhill from the ponies, check out the free petting zoo, open from late April through August. The baby goats delight children by trotting up to be petted, and the piglets play chase. Meanwhile, lambs are bleating, ducks are quacking, turkeys are gobbling, and llamas are, well, chewing and staring.

HEY KIDS! While you're at the petting zoo, peek through the window at the hens sitting on their nests. Next time you eat eggs—fried, scrambled or hard-boiled—think about those hard-working birds. If you count all the chickens in the United States, they lay about 7 billion eggs every month! That's about 20 eggs a month for each one. So be sure to say "thanks"!

802 Mukilteo Blvd., Everett

 Free; pool session $1.50 children under 17, $2 adults

Varies seasonally

425/257–8300; 425/257–8312 swimming pool

 1 and up

Don't have a pet at home? Here's your chance to try one out. The park always has lots of cuddly rabbits and animal babies, some for sale. The others can be adopted for a weekend—the park supplies the cage and food, you supply $10 and the TLC. It's a great way to teach kids how to care for a pet without the long-term commitment.

On warm days, let the little ones cool their heels in the wading pool. The full-size swimming pool has diving boards for older kids; a small slide and rope swing for younger ones. Call ahead for the daily schedule. With 100 acres of fun surrounded by forests of towering pines, this park is sure to make your family's day!

EATS FOR KIDS
Pack up a picnic and grab one of the park's many grills for a family feast. You can also buy your lunch already cooked at the **hot dog stand**, which also sells popcorn and drinks.

GETTING THERE Tucked away in Everett, Lake Forest Park is relatively undiscovered, except by locals. From Seattle, take I-5 north to Exit 192 (Broadway). Then take the second exit ramp to the right (41st Street). Turn right on 41st Street and drive up the hillside, where the road becomes Mukilteo Boulevard. The park is at the top, on the left.

LINCOLN PARK

I imagine floating the day away in a heated, outdoor saltwater pool, while looking out at a crystal-clear view of Puget Sound through a transparent wall. Now, stop imagining and head for Lincoln Park, across the West Seattle Bridge from the mainland. The picture-perfect setting captures a truly Northwest experience.

The whole family can enjoy the blissful buoyancy of swimming in Colman Pool's 500,000 gallons of salt water, drawn directly from Puget Sound, then filtered and chlorinated. The sight of the 50-foot corkscrew slide makes most kids' eyes pop out, but remind them they must pass a 40-yard swim test before they're allowed to spiral down. If your little tyke is happier splashing about in shallow water, a huge wading pool on the north end of the park is open from the end of June through August.

If you're bringing a stroller, park in the south lot on Fauntleroy Way, which opens onto a flat bicycle and walking trail down to the pool. This popular path draws lots of mom

GETTING THERE From Seattle, take I–5 to the West Seattle Bridge exit. Cross the bridge and follow Fauntleroy Way toward the Vashon Ferry. Lincoln Park is just north of the ferry dock.

KEEP IN MIND Be aware that the Colman Pool has no graduated steps for entry. The built-in ladders are somewhat treacherous, so for safety's sake it's better to have one adult hand a tot or baby to another adult in the water. You can check out tiny life jackets on the deck at no charge; you'll find lots of toys and foam "noodles" floating around as well. For those who need help getting in and out of this pool, a mechanical lift-seat is available.

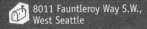 8011 Fauntleroy Way S.W.,
West Seattle

 206/684-4075

 Free; Colman Pool $2.50
adults, $1.75 ages 1–18;
$1 corkscrew slide

Park 4 AM–11:30 PM; pool daily, mid-
May–mid-Sep; public swimming 12–7

1 and up

and dad bicyclists pulling baby trailers behind them. If your kids can handle steeper slopes, park in the north lot and take any of the trails through the woods, all of which lead to Colman Pool. Along the way, stop and enjoy the fragrant forests of cedars and Madronas, dramatic hillside views of the Sound, horseshoe pits, picnic areas galore, tennis courts, and two children's play areas.

The southern playground draws younger kids with its jumbo-size sandbox and challenging climbing, sliding, and swinging equipment. It also has an extra-special attraction that has been known to light up the eyes of the most jaded teenager—a pulley-and-cable-operated rope swing. You hop on, then ride down a slope. Even the occasional mom and dad have been spotted doing Tarzan imitations.

EATS FOR KIDS Throughout the park are plenty of picnic areas and grills; a picnic area is also reserved for those who have paid to go swimming. And bring your kite along! For indoor dining, the **Saffron Cow** (9261 45th Ave. S.W., tel. 206/923–1729) serves yummy deli sandwiches and full meals. Like that chair you're sitting on? You can take it home with you—the tables and chairs are antique, and they're all for sale!

MARYMOOR PARK

44

It's easy to see why Marymoor Park is the most popular park in King County. It's not only a great place to picnic or fly a kite, but it's a perfect spot for rock-climbing, model airplane–zooming, velodrome bike–racing, museum-exploring, fishing, pea-patch gardening, and off-leash dog romping.

This green oasis of activity sprawls over a square mile east of Lake Washington, across the Evergreen Point Floating Bridge. As you drive into the park, you'll pass the old Willowmoore Farm windmill, left over from the park's earlier days as a dairy farm. The mill once sat on the Sammamish River, before the Army Corps of Engineers moved it to its present site. The windmill's builder, John Clise, also erected a hunting lodge, a small mansion that now houses the Marymoor Museum of Eastside History. It may be hard to get the kids indoors on a sunny day, but once inside, they'll find that this park has been a popular spot for a long time. Archaeologists have dug up stone tools here used by Indians 11,000 years ago.

KEEP IN MIND In the summertime, the park hosts a variety of special events, from horse shows to free outdoor cinemas. The best-loved event is the Heritage Festival, which brings history to life every Fourth of July weekend. In addition to reenactments of Civil War encampments and Oregon Trail travels, a ballgame is played, in period costumes, by 1860s rules.

6046 West Lake Sammamish
Parkway N.E., Redmond

206/205-8751

Free

Daily 8 AM–dusk

All ages

After the history lesson, take the family on a hike along the Interpretive Trail, where much of the scenery remains unchanged from the time of its earlier inhabitants. This area is a wildlife preserve, home to lots of critters and birds. The trail is about 2 miles long, ending in a dirt-and-gravel pathway to the park entrance. If you're pushing a stroller, drive to the trail parking lot and start out on the paved path, which leads to a raised boardwalk. Turn back before you reach the rougher trail.

Whatever your age, it's hard to run out of things to do at Marymoor. Tots can swing and climb at the playground; older kids can drop their fishing poles into Lake Sammamish, race their bikes along the banked velodrome track, climb the 45-foot artificial rock, or fly their remote-control airplanes. Or just have a picnic. Then go fly a kite.

EATS FOR KIDS

Picnic tables and grills abound in the park. Dine in at the **Red Robin** at Redmond Town Center (7597 170th Ave. N.E., tel. 425/895–1870) for kid-friendly meals, from noodles to burgers to sandwiches. The **Family Pancake House** (17621 Redmond Way, tel. 425/883–0922), outside the park, serves tasty hotcakes, waffles, and sandwiches, all at great prices.

HEY KIDS! In the park, you'll notice four huge mounds. Those were once trash piles, mainly consisting of empty mussel and clam shells left from the Indians who lived in the area thousands of years ago. These mounds help explain how local tribes lived. For example, the dirt here is darker in the park than in surrounding areas. That's because so many salmon were prepared for eating here that the soil became oily. Imagine what clues your garbage would reveal about you!

MOSQUITO FLEET

Animal lovers need look no further for a ride on the chilly waters off Puget Sound to watch the antics of playful orcas from the decks of a whale-watching boat. These lively, inquisitive mammals seem to think boats are playground equipment, swimming around and underneath, then popping up on the other side. Seeing one of these huge but graceful creatures leap out of the water, then slide back into its watery world, perhaps with a bouncing baby in tow, is a thrilling sight!

The Mosquito Fleet is based at the Everett port, a half hour north of Seattle. Boarding starts at 8 AM on these smooth, fast passenger vessels with open-air upper decks; arrive early for a window seat. The boat leaves at 8:30, then winds around enchanting green islands and through beautiful Deception Pass on its way to the San Juan Islands. That's where the engines are shut down and the boat drifts into whale territory. Operators of local whale-

EATS FOR KIDS You're welcome to bring your own food aboard the Mosquito Fleet, but the boat's **snack bar** serves nachos, hot dogs, burgers, and sandwiches.

KEEP IN MIND Although watching whales and other sea creatures is a thrilling adventure, eight hours on a boat is a long day for a pre-schooler. Unless you have a docile toddler who can nap easily and be amused for hours with books and toys, the little ones may be happier at home.

1724 W. Marine View Drive, Everett

 $79 peak, $59 off-peak adults; $39.50 peak, $29.50 off-peak children 3–17

 Mid-Apr–mid-Oct., departs 8:30 and returns 5 PM, days vary

 425/252–6800; www.whalewatching.com

6 and up

watching cruises are usually careful not to disturb the whale population. The playful whales themselves initiate the close encounters.

Naturalists on board the Mosquito Fleet enrich the experience through quizzes and educational demonstrations, such as putting one hand in 45-degree water and the other inside a piece of whale blubber in the same water. It's much better than a lecture about how whales endure swimming in the frigid Puget Sound.

Not every cruise has an orca encounter, but about 80 percent do. The staff can tell you before you board if whales have been spotted that morning. Even if you don't see any whales, you'll see lots of other sea creatures. Frequent sightings include lounging harbor seals, nesting bald eagles, and sleek blue herons.

HEY KIDS! The whales you see swimming around the San Juan islands are called orcas. Like humans, they tend to travel in families, or pods. Three large families of whales—the L, K and J pods—spend their summers in the Pacific Northwest. Scientists can tell all the whales apart, and each one has a name—such as Granny, Oreo, and Rascal. What name would you choose for a whale?

MUKILTEO LIGHTHOUSE

The Mukilteo Lighthouse, just north of Seattle, has guided boats safely through Puget Sound for about 100 years. These days, it's automatic. But in the earlier days, a keeper with a kerosene lantern did the honors.

During the guided tour, volunteers are stationed at the bottom and top of a steep, winding 36-step climb into the 30-foot-tall tower. They eagerly provide information about the history and structure of the lighthouse and answer questions about how it works. At the top, the original lens, built in Paris in 1852, is still in use as well as the bulb that illuminates it. Kids will get a science lesson on how prisms enable the lens to make such a small light shine 12 miles across the water. Be sure to take in the postcard-panoramic view of the Olympics and Cascades, plus nearby Whidbey and Camano islands.

EATS FOR KIDS Several grills and picnic tables are scattered along the beach. For delicious clams, shrimp, or fish from an outside take-out window, try **Ivar's** (710 Front St., Mukilteo, tel. 206/742–6180) next to the ferry dock. You can carry your meal to the beach and munch away as you watch the waves lap and the ferry boats glide across the Sound.

In the ground-level displays, you can examine a large lens taken from another lighthouse, the original Mukilteo Lighthouse log book, and a copy of the peace treaty signed here in 1855 by dozens of local Native American leaders and the Washington territorial governor. After the tour, head over to the beach, one of the widest and sandiest around. Kids have plenty of room to run, and even dogs are welcome. It's also a favorite local spot for catching the sunset.

In mid-August, the city turns on the charm for the annual Mukilteo Lighthouse Festival. The fun lasts for three days and includes food, arts, and a parade. In December, the lighthouse puts on its holiday best, outshining its usual glow with a blanket of holiday lights.

KEEP IN MIND
If you have a lighthouse buff in your family, take the Mukilteo ferry, right next to the light-house, over to Whidbey Island and drive about 25 miles north on Highway 525 to Fort Casey State Park. Here you can tour the brick-and-stucco Admiralty Head Light-house (tel. 360/679–7391). Get an early start and you can easily fit both lighthouses into one day's outing.

HEY KIDS! Many years ago, when the coastline lacked the many towns and buildings that exist today, lighthouses were built along the beaches to help sailors figure out where they were and keep them away from rocky shorelines. The light-houses were painted different patterns and colors and each one was given its own special signal pattern—Mukilteo's is a two-seconds-on, three-seconds-off flash— so mariners could check their chart to see which one they were passing at night.

MUSEUM OF FLIGHT

41

The planes here won't take flight, but your kids' imaginations will soar as they walk through this fascinating museum, just south of town at Boeing Field/King County International Airport. Fittingly, it was the site of Seattle's first powered airplane flight.

Early aviation history takes the stage in the Red Barn, a restored 1909 building that served as Boeing's original manufacturing plant. Exhibits here include a 1917 Curtiss "Jenny" biplane and a working model of the Wright Brothers' wind tunnel. The glass-and-steel Great Gallery showcases the concept of flight all the way from mythology to the space era. Historic airplanes suspend dramatically from a sky-high ceiling, as if poised to take flight at a moment's notice. A working replica of Boeing's first airplane—a World War II Corsair—and a U.S space program exhibit enrich the experience. At the Challenger Learning Center, kids can participate in space flight problem-solving skills. You can also tour the first presidential airplane, a Boeing VC–137B, which was delivered to Dwight Eisenhower in 1959.

KEEP IN MIND Don't worry if your kids aren't aviation aficionados because they're sure to find plenty to interest them here. From the space station to the crafts workshops, the museum has put lots of energy into stimulating inquisitive young minds.

HEY KIDS! As you walk through the museum, you'll see lots of airplanes hanging from the ceiling. If you tried that at home the planes would fall right through your floor! After all, just one of those planes—the Douglas DC-3—weighs in at 18,000 pounds. So how do they do it? The museum's webbed ceiling is made up of twelve 30-ton steel panels, plenty strong enough to hold the 20 airplanes suspended above your head. So don't worry—they're not coming down!

9404 E. Marginal Way S.

 $9.50 adult, $5 ages 5–17

 206/764–5720;
www.museumofflight.org

F–T 10–5, Th 10–9

7 and up

Videos and hands-on exhibits keep youngsters busy and happy, including a nine-seat Flight Simulator. For many kids, the favorite is the International Space Station, where audio and video presentations describe life in orbit for the astronauts from 16 nations. In this topsy-turvy home away from home, the sleeping bags are on the walls, the suction toilet is on the ceiling, and nothing is quite as it seems! As any kid will tell you, this exhibit is out of this world.

The Museum of Flight hosts terrific workshops for kids and parents every Saturday and Sunday. Sign up when you arrive; it's included in your admission fee. Although children under 6 are permitted, the program is really geared toward the lower elementary level. Kids listen to a brief lesson on the day's topic, then the hands-on fun begins. They might make kites, build rockets, or fold paper airplanes. Classes are held several times a day, so call ahead for the schedule.

EATS FOR KIDS You'll find plenty of salads, sandwiches, pasta and fun at the museum's large **Wings Café** (206/762–4418). It's open the same hours as the Museum of Flight. Drive up to First Street for delicious home-made sandwiches, pies, and cakes at the **Alki Bakery** (5700 1st S., tel. 206/762–5700).

MUSEUM OF HISTORY AND INDUSTRY

Great balls of fire! That's all you would have seen if you'd looked up at the Seattle skies on the sunny afternoon of June 6, 1889. By the time you finish looking at MOHAI's exhibit on The Great Fire, you'll be checking your clothes for ashes.

The museum recreates everything but the flames to tell the tale of a workshop blaze that ended up razing an entire city. Kids can push buttons to hear the fascinating story or watch a video filled with historic photos and quirky details—like how the firemen's pants caught fire. Flip-over flaps reveal pictures of Seattle buildings and streets before and after the fire. On display are some original wooden water mains and old firefighting equipment, from helmets to buckets to a fire-hose cart. Remnants salvaged from the fire really bring the experience to life for children, such as charred spoons, dolls, cups, and plates. Luckily, no one died, so no sad explanations are required.

MOHAI also includes such unusual collections as colorful ship figureheads—the hand-carved

HEY KIDS! Lots of things were working against Seattle the day the Great Fire started in 1889. The fire chief was out of town, the water pressure was too low to fill the fire hoses, a wind was fanning the flames, and a heat wave had dried out the city. On top of all that, almost the entire town was built of wood! Seattle burned to the ground, but its citizens didn't sit around and fret. In just a year, 130 new buildings were built, made from brick and stone, not wood!

 2700 24th Ave. E.

 $5.50 adult, $3 ages 6–12, $1 ages 2–5

 Daily 10–5

206/324–1126

7 and up

wooden, often mythical, figures once attached to the prows of boats—dating from 1878. You'll also find extensive collections of old shoes, from 19th-century baby booties to men's wingtips, and clothes of every type.

Perhaps the oddest exhibit at MOHAI is "Salmon Stakes," which highlights the salmon canning industry. The canning process was transformed in 1909 by an automatic salmon-butchering machine invented in Seattle. Kids can try their hand at "butchering" a large plastic fish. Flashing lights challenge them to match the speed of an apprentice butcher, then an expert, and finally the revolutionary cannery machine. Kind of strange, but kids love it!

Don't miss the diorama illustrating the landing of the Denny Party, Seattle's founders, at Alki Beach. With just a push of a button, kids can hear the story of Seattle's earliest days!

KEEP IN MIND If you have very young children, it's a good idea to time the "Seattle 1880s" exhibit halfway through your visit. A "While You Look" area, set up with children's books and comfy pillows, gives tots a break while keeping them within eyesight as parents stroll through the "town."

EATS FOR KIDS
Pack a lunch and sit on the patio outside the museum, overlooking the woods and lovely Lake Washington. At **Hop-In Grocery** (2605 22nd Ave. E., tel. 206/323–4518) you can eat great soups and sandwiches in the deli.

NAVAL UNDERSEA MUSEUM

Underneath the waves, a dark, watery world exists where we humans are out of our element. But that's never stopped us from taking the plunge, and the technology we've used to explore the deepest seas gets the limelight at this museum.

Several exhibits illuminate the underwater world, with plenty of hands-on activities and videos to enrich the experience. The Diving Technology section shows just how far technology has evolved since the odd-looking diving bells and aqualungs. Examples include such high-tech equipment as armored diving suits, which let divers plunge 1,000 feet below the surface, and the remote-controlled diving sub, which grabs torpedoes from the ocean's floor.

Young naval buffs will reach new depths of joy at the Outside Exhibits, where they can see partial and complete submarines. How low did they go? The Navy research sub *Deep*

GETTING THERE Take the ferryboat from Seattle to Bremerton, then take Highway 3 north to Rte 308. Take a right on on Rte. 308 and follow the signs to Keyport, then watch for signs to the museum.

HEY KIDS! A Dutchman named Cornelis Drebbel built the first submarine in 1620. The first one used in war was the *Turtle*, designed by David Bushnell to be used against the British in the Revolutionary War. But his sub wasn't quite able to sink an enemy warship. The first time that happened was in the Civil War, when the Confederate *Hunley* sub destroyed a Union ship. Today's super-fast subs use nuclear power.

610 Dowell St., Keyport

 Free

 Jun–Sep, daily 10–4; Oct–May, W–M 10–4

360/396-4148;
www-num.kpt.nuwc.navy.mil

7 and up

Quest dove 8,000 feet under the sea, and the *Trieste II* reached 20,000 feet—almost as deep as Mount Everest is high! In the Torpedo Technology section, you'll find the most comprehensive collection of torpedoes in the country. The Keyport submarine base was established in 1914 as the Pacific Coast Torpedo Station; today, it's one of two divisions of the Naval Undersea Warfare Center.

If kids get restless at the warfare exhibits, take them to the Ocean Environment exhibit, which focuses on the differences between the 70 percent of our planet under water and the part we live on. Kids can do a buoyancy experiment, use a microscope to examine tiny sea creatures, and listen to a recording of just how noisy the undersea world is. You can't find a better museum for children who love subs and diving.

EATS FOR KIDS In Silverdale, **Red Robin** (10455 Silverdale Way N.W., tel. 360/698-4822) serves up everything from grilled cheese to spaghetti at reasonable prices. Nearby **Kitsap Mall** (10315 Silverdale Way N.W., tel. 360/698-2555) has a food court and a kiddie play area that includes Periscope Place, an "undersea" adventureland—a perfect after-museum stop.

NORDIC HERITAGE MUSEUM

History comes alive with vibrant exhibits and events at this museum dedicated to collecting and preserving Scandinavian art. Great care has gone into recreating the experiences of early Scandinavian settlers who came to the Northwest. One exhibit enables you to ride on a fishing boat, complete with nets, uneven flooring, steering wheel, and ramps; another takes you outside an early immigrant's drab tenement, with laundry flapping on the line.

As you stroll through the museum, divided into five galleries—one for each Scandinavian country—you'll walk through replicas of early towns, lined with barbershops, drugstores, post offices, saloons, and Danish bakeries. Look through the windows and look at the astounding details—in the barbershop, you'll see hair clippings on the floor. There's something in each exhibit that appeals to children, such as colorful textiles, cherished china, books and Bibles, photographs and a myriad of other treasures brought from the Old Country to enrich life in a new land.

HEY KIDS! As you walk around the wooden deck of the boat room, modeled after the ships that brought thousands of immigrants to the United States in the late 1800s, think how exciting it must have been for those newcomers to see the Statue of Liberty welcoming them to their new home. Walk down the ramp and onto the "island" and imagine that you've just spent weeks crossing the ocean on a crowded, smelly ship. Land looks pretty good, doesn't it?

 3014 N.W. 67th St.

 Free

206/789–5707;
www.nordicmuseum.com

T–Sa 10–4, Su 12–4

All ages

This three-floor museum does an excellent job of pulling visitors into its stories. In addition to the life-size replicas, clever sound effects breathe life into the exhibits. As you pass a farm, cows moo and horses clomp. Babies cry on the boat approaching Ellis Island. And a train whistles as it chugs toward the Northwest.

Even the youngest visitor will find something of interest, though the self-guided exhibits are primarily targeted at ages 8 and up. If you do bring a little one in a stroller, elevators help navigate the three floors. Best bets for keeping a young child's attention are the first-floor Dream of America exhibit, filled with bright colors and many sound effects, and the fishing-boat exhibit on the second floor.

All in all, this museum is a fascinating and fun history lesson, which will amuse your children and you.

EATS FOR KIDS A snack stand on the beach sells hot dogs, burgers, popcorn and ice cream. Next to the park, **Little Coney** (8001 Seaview N.W., tel. 206/782–6598) serves up fish and chips, hamburgers, or clam chowder. For an authentic Ballard-style treat, try the Danish kringle or other goodies at **Larsen's Original Danish Bakery** (8000 24th Ave. N.W., tel. 206/782–8285).

KEEP IN MIND While you're in Ballard, visit Golden Gardens for a little playful respite. The equipment here is mainly for preschoolers. In the shade of huge pines, the slides and swings never get too hot for tender skin. For older kids, the attraction is the long, wide, sandy beach. If the water's too chilly for the little ones, try the creek that empties onto the sand, which creates a warm, shallow pool that's perfect for splashing and jumping.

NORTHWEST OUTDOOR CENTER

A crisp, sunny day in Seattle is hard to beat, and what better way to spend it than kayaking around Lake Union in a sleek, water-level boat. You can even use the experience to build a little family teamwork, with two to a kayak and everybody pulling their own weight.

On still days, the lake is a tranquil pool of blue with a breathtaking view of Seattle, with the Space Needle rising like an exclamation point just north of downtown. You can paddle around the hundreds of houseboats moored on Lake Union, one of which starred in the movie *Sleepless in Seattle*. You'll see everything from quirky tugboats to ultra-luxury yachts. You'll even see a planned houseboat community, with homes that look more like sprawling condos than humble boats. Start a family conversation about what it would be like to live in a floating home.

With older children, you can paddle all the way to Lake Washington and back, about

EATS FOR KIDS China **Harbor Restaurant** (2040 Westlake N., tel. 206/286–2688), two buildings down from NWOC, serves a variety of noodle dishes. Toward downtown on Westlake, **Buca di Beppo** (701 9th N., tel. 206/244–2288) serves family-sized portions of Italian fare.

KEEP IN MIND You can get a closer look at houseboats on the Discover Houseboating Tour (tel. 206/322–9157). Seattle's "Houseboat Lady," Jeri Callahan, is a retired teacher with a knack for entertaining kids. A houseboat-dweller herself, she knows the ins and outs of life on Lake Union. The tour costs $25 per person, with a minimum of three people per trip, and usually leaves the dock at 10 AM April through October.

2100 Westlake Ave. N. Ste. 1

 206/281-9694; www.nwoc.com

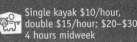 Single kayak $10/hour, double $15/hour; $20–$30 4 hours midweek

Apr–Sep, M–F 10–8, Sa–Su 9–6; Oct–Mar, W–M 10–6

5 and up

an hour each way. And if Mount Rainier is "out"—which depends on nearby clouds—the view is a real treat. In just an hour, you can paddle north past Gas Works Park (see #52); then circle around the Kalakala, a historic, Art Deco–era Puget Sound ferry.

Life jackets come in small sizes, but before you bring a toddler on board, be sure your child is patient enough to sit in one spot for at least an hour. Then point your craft toward the city and off you go.

NWOC is tucked away at dock level, right under your feet at Julie's Landing. To get there, follow Westlake Avenue north along the lake. When you see the China Harbor restaurant, pull into the next parking lot on your right, near the tall waterfront clock. You can walk downstairs or take the elevator.

HEY KIDS! How would you like to live on a houseboat, with a lake as your backyard and trout as your neighbors? That's what hundreds of families in Seattle do! Just like any other neighborhood, some of the houses are plain and others are fancy. Since the houseboats have no real yards, many families hang plants all over their boats. On land or water, there's no place like home!

NORTHWEST PUPPET CENTER

There's nothing quite like a puppet show to keep a roomful of kids on the edge of their seats. And no one pulls the strings better than the talented Carter Family Marionettes, who have worked their magic around the world for decades.

The Carters and touring puppeteers perform October through May here, in a renovated church in the University District. The shows vary from such beloved children's fables as "The Tale of Peter Rabbit" and folk tales from the far reaches of the globe to historical stories and even opera. The troupes are award-winning performers from around the world; the Carters, who have trained with master puppeteers from Romania, Sicily, and China, have landed some top honors themselves. The artists are incredibly gifted at bringing the puppets to life and at interacting with children.

The Carters choose a variety of shows to appeal to younger and older children, and they'll make age recommendations over the phone. The shows are short enough to keep attention

EATS FOR KIDS Pack a lunch and eat it before the show in the covered picnic area. Kids can swing, slide, and climb on the playground to burn off energy before they have to go inside and sit still. If you'd rather eat after the show, walk up 92nd, turn left on Roosevelt, and walk two blocks to the **Maple Leaf Grill** (8909 Roosevelt Way N.E., tel. 206/632–7060) for a tasty eclectic menu, including sandwiches and Andouille sausage stew. Don't miss the bread pudding.

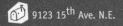 9123 15th Ave. N.E.

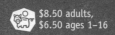 $8.50 adults, $6.50 ages 1–16

 F–Sa evenings; weekend matinees

206/523–2579; www.nwpuppet.org

3–11

spans from wandering—less than an hour for performances for the youngest audiences. The colorful and engaging puppets vary from intricately carved wooden marionettes to beautifully crafted hand puppets. Most of the shows include live music and singing, and children are encouraged to join in.

In addition to theater seats, a large carpeted floor invites youngsters to sprawl out on their tummies and stare wide-eyed at the stage. After the show, kids can come up to the stage to "talk" to the puppets. Up close and personal with Peter Rabbit? It's a preschooler's dream come true.

On your way out, take in the museum exhibits, which chronicle the history of puppetry, from antique toy theaters to dozens of marionettes from past shows. If Dmitri Carter is around, he'll bring some out and put them through their paces.

KEEP IN MIND
If you plan on seeing a lot of puppet shows, now or in the future, pick up a Puppet Pass. You can get a four-show pass for $22 for a child and $30 for an adult, or a six-show pass for $30 and $42.

HEY KIDS! Puppets have been around since around 5 BC when they were created in Greece. At that time, though, puppet shows were meant for grown-ups. The strings on the puppets showed humans were being controlled by mysterious fates. But don't worry! Now everyone knows now that kids and puppets go hand in hand.

NORTHWEST TREK WILDLIFE PARK

E ver wonder how the animals at the zoo must feel, being stared at all day long? Well, at this backward zoo, it's the animals that do the staring—at the humans, confined to their tram cars.

The hourlong ride takes you through 300 acres of free-roam habitat. In the spring, don't be surprised to spot a mother moose and her gangly calf just outside your window. Also meandering about the grasslands and wetlands are elk, bighorn sheep, caribou, mountain goats, deer, Sandhill cranes, and Mallard ducks. All the animals are native Northwesterners. Little ones will get a kick out of spotting the critters from the tram window. Older children can learn little-known facts about the animals—everything from camouflage to mating behavior. The drivers occasionally stop so you can get a close-up look at animals that approach the tram.

The rest of the park consists of individual habitat areas with overlooks. An amazing

EATS FOR KIDS Pack a picnic lunch and eat at the tables outdoors or in the heated picnic pavilion. You can also gather around the fireplace in the park's **Fir Bough Café** and eat sandwiches and other light fare.

HEY KIDS! Have you ever heard the expression "like a deer in headlights"? It means someone looks scared but is standing perfectly still, just like a deer does when a car's headlights shine in its eyes. If the deer is frightened, why does it just stand there? Many predators, like the meat-eating dinosaurs in the movie *Jurassic Park*, can only see their prey if it's moving. So the deer thinks it's safe, as long as it stands still!

 11610 Trek Dr. E., Eatonville

 $8.75 adults, $6 ages 5–17, $4 ages 3–4

Opens daily 9:30 AM, closing time varies

360/832-6117; www.nwtrek.org

 1 and up

variety of animals such as gray wolves, grizzly bears, black bears, raccoons, beavers, skunks, bobcats, cougars, bald eagles, owls, and porcupines happily share the grounds. There's a lot of walking, so you might want to keep the little ones in their strollers most of the time. If they start becoming restless, let them run in the grassy areas scattered throughout the park. They can prance along the circular path of stumps of varying heights, across from the Forest Theater. Another good place to let the tots loose is the underwater-observation area, which is mostly enclosed and has no railings or high ledges.

For younger children, the park's discovery center provides nature crafts and other hands-on experiences. Special tours, though pricey, are a real treat. A favorite, the Free-Roaming Area Keeper Tour, brings you within an arm's length of bison, moose, and caribou.

GETTING THERE From Seattle, head south on I–5, then take Exit 154A (I–405 north to Renton). Drive 2 miles, then take Exit 2 (SR 167 south to Renton and Auburn). Drive 20 miles south on SR 167, exit on SR 512 (west to Puyallup). From there, drive 3 miles, then exit at SR 161 (to South Hill and Eatonville). Turn left at the light, and you have 17 more miles to go. Northwest Trek is on the left.

ODYSSEY CONTEMPORARY MARITIME MUSEUM

Water, water everywhere. Especially at the Odyssey, where dozens of exhibits on fishing and shipping focus on the waterways that have shaped Seattle's destiny. Lots of high-tech bells and whistles keep kids interested, and protecting the environment is a major theme.

Some exhibits are just plain fun! For most youngsters, the highlight is the virtual sea kayaking. You sit in the boat, listen to the kayaking instructions, then grab the oars and select a destination. As you paddle, the front of the craft appears on the screen. But look out for obstacles! A similar exhibit lets kids "steer" a container ship to the dock in busy Elliott Bay. They can also sit at the controls of a crane and move cargo from ship to shore.

In between virtual adventures, soak up some science and history, such as how the Puget Sound was formed. You'll learn about many of the animals that live in local waterways, from crabs and clams in the tideflats to orcas and seals in the open seas. Kids can take

HEY KIDS! For a fish, the Puget Sound salmon has quite an interesting life. It's born in a stream, then hides until it grows big enough to travel to the ocean. That's when it swims into the Sound, where it stays for awhile before heading out to sea. A year or more later, that same salmon comes back to the Sound, rests again, then leaps up the fish ladders and streams to the very spot where it was born. Why does it return? To spawn new babies, which start the cycle all over again.

 2205 Alaskan Way, Pier 66

 $6.75 adults;
$4.50 ages 5–18

M–Sa 10–5, Su 12–5

206/623–2120

5–11

interactive quizzes to see how much they've learned. Upstairs, a big chart shows all the different types of boats that come into the Puget Sound, including an updated list of ships arriving and leaving each day. Peer through the binoculars to see how many you can spot.

On your way through the museum, take a break and catch one of the short movies that run throughout the day. One film takes you along the Inside Passage route, from Puget Sound to Glacier Bay, Alaska, which miners used to make their way to the gold fields. Another takes you on a train trip from Ohio to Seattle, where cargo is loaded onto a ship for a voyage across the Pacific.

As you leave, stroll out on the fishing dock for a great view of Puget Sound. By now, you'll feel like an old salt!

EATS FOR KIDS Catch the trolley and head south of Odyssey, where you'll find two local landmarks that serve fresh, tasty seafood with kids' portions: **Ivar's Acres of Clams** (Pier 54, tel. 206/624–6852) and **The Fisherman's Restaurant & Bar** (Pier 57, tel. 206/623–3500).

KEEP IN MIND If you bring children under 5 to this museum, a couple of downstairs exhibits will grab their attention if they start to get jittery. For climbing and make-believe fun, look for the ride-on, fabric tugboats; the eight-person lifeboat; and the "Kid Skiff," which has life vests to try on and a wheel to turn. They may also enjoy the color and movement in the short movies, which run throughout the day in several areas of the museum.

OLYMPIC GAME FARM

If you've never experienced yak breath, you don't know what you're missing! Up-close and personal is the name of the game at this unusual farm, where free-roaming beasts such as zebras, elk, bison, and yaks poke their heads inside your car windows and beg for bread.

Not all the critters are running around loose. Kids can throw bread to the brown bears lurking behind a fence. Don't be surprised to see a few of them grin and wave back. Some of the bears on Lloyd and Catherine Beebe's 87-acre farm are veteran actors, trained for movies and TV shows. The Beebes have provided animals for such Disney productions as *The Incredible Journey* and *Davy Crockett* for many years.

So stock up on bread before you come or buy it at the entrance. The inhabitants are expecting it, and watching them munch is what the thrill is all about. Whatever you do, don't forget your camera. If you have animal-shy little ones, better wait till they're

GETTING THERE To get to the Beebes' spread, take the ferry to Bainbridge Island, drive north on S.R. 305 toward Hood Canal, then follow S.R. 104 onto U.S. Highway 101. Turn off at the Sequim (pronounced "squim") Ave. exit and watch for the zebra billboard.

EATS FOR KIDS If your own little herd is hungry, you can get most anything they want at **Alice's Restaurant**, a snack bar inside the game farm. You'll also find plenty of choices if you choose to eat outside the farm in Sequim. **The 101 Diner** (4th & Washington Streets, tel. 360/683–3388) is a blast from the past, with mini jukeboxes at each table and burger, pizza, and pasta diner fare. If Mom and Dad are craving seafood, **The Three Crabs** (11 Three Crabs Road, tel. 360/683–4264) serves it up with a stunning view of the ocean and mountains.

1423 Ward Rd., Sequim

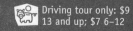 Driving tour only: $9
13 and up; $7 6–12

 Driving tours daily 9 AM; walking
tours Memorial Day–Labor Day

360/683–4295;
www.olygamefarm.com

 2 and up

older to visit this farm. An in-your-face bison can be a bit intimidating, even from the safety of the back seat.

The guided walking tour, conducted only from Memorial Day through Labor Day, leads you through the caged side of the farm, which includes several endangered species. You'll see wolves, tigers, lions, coyotes, and cougars—critters you probably wouldn't want nudging your shoulder or your SUV. If the kids haven't had their fill of one-on-one animal encounters, take them to the small petting area, open only in the summertime. Then you can drool over some of the tastiest kinds of fish in the Northwest, swimming safely and soundly in the farm's aquarium. In the Studio Barn, kids will enjoy seeing the sets where much of the filming was done for Walt Disney Studios.

It's a bit of a hike from Seattle. But this is one beastly experience your family shouldn't miss.

HEY KIDS! Take a good look at the white rhinoceros. It's the biggest kind of rhino, and there aren't too many white rhinos left in the world. You might wonder how this dark gray animal got its name. When it rolls in the mud, which rhinos love to do, the mud looks kind of white when it dries. The name—like the mud—just stuck!

PACIFIC RIM BONSAI COLLECTION

Stately trees stretch their gnarled limbs toward the sky, as some of them have done for hundreds of years, in this "forest." But don't worry about craning your neck. Dozens of these teensy-weensy, painstakingly trained miniature trees, only a couple of feet tall, surround you as you walk. The garden is small enough that young children won't get too bored, especially since they can explore paths and try out benches.

To honor its Asian customers, the Weyerhaeuser lumber company created this exhibit of living art, at Weyerhaeuser Co.'s headquarters 20 miles south of Seattle. The ancient tree-growing technique of bonsai (Japanese for "planting in a shallow container") began in China, caught on in Korea, and was popularized in Japan. Generations have tended the many trees in this collection. Some have won awards and have appeared in magazines and books. Each tree is labeled with the type of tree, its age, and artist. Bonsai growers are called artists, not gardeners.

KEEP IN MIND While you're in the neighborhood, check out the spectacular Rhododendron Species Botanical Garden (2525 S. 336th St., Federal Way; tel. 253/838–4646), which is privately owned but shares a courtyard—and hours—with Pacific Rim Bonsai. More than 10,000 rhodys—80 percent of the types known in the world—adorn this 24-acre garden. The rhododendrons only bloom from about February through June, but plenty of other flowering plants and trees are here to admire. Admission is $3.50 for adults; free for kids 12 and under.

33663 Weyerhaeuser Way S.,
Federal Way

 Free

 Mar–May 10 AM–4 PM F–W;
Jun–Feb 11 AM–4 PM Sa–W

 8 and up

253/924–5206

Grab a brochure and take a self-guided walk through the Pacific Rim Bonsai Collection, or show up at noon any Sunday for a free guided tour. No reservations are needed. From May to September, you can catch a bonsai lecture every other Sunday in the courtyard. But this is probably more information than most youngsters want, unless you happen to have a botany-bent teen.

Any time of year is a good time to check out these tiny trees. For the best viewing, visit in the springtime, when the new blossoms pop open, or in the fall, when the branches are cloaked in splendid reds and yellows.

EATS FOR KIDS
Bring the family to **Burger Express** (32805 Pacific Hwy. S., tel. 253/874–2701) with its kid-friendly menu including burgers, chicken strips, fish, and shrimp. Another great choice is **Café de Paris** (33606 Pacific Hwy. S., tel. 253/661–3721), where you can chow down on pasta salad, soups, and half or whole sandwiches.

HEY KIDS! Bonsai trees are really works of art. The artist gets an idea, picks out a tree, then carefully trains it by trimming it, feeding it, and using wire supports to create tricky angles. Like paintings, these little trees are designed to suggest different moods. See if you can spot some examples: Straight, upright bonsais are supposed to represent tranquility and simplicity, angled ones show grace and movement, and cascading bonsais suggest strength and willpower. Look at them closely and see if you can "read" their moods.

PACIFIC SCIENCE CENTER

Please touch! That's the motto at Pacific Science Center, where all the exhibits are designed for little explorers.

At this longtime Seattle attraction, in the shadow of the Space Needle, the favorite hangout of kids 5 and up is the dinosaur area, where robotic models of the lumbering beasts seem to spring to life. These robotic dinos give kids a thrill as they move and roar in their tropical environment. Question-and-answer cards, written with young readers in mind, explain various theories of why these giants disappeared.

After watching the dinosaurs, move to the 600-gallon saltwater tide pool. Children as young as 3 can touch the mechanized colorful crabs and other small marine animals that inhabit the shores of Puget Sound. In the Animal Attractions exhibit, they can observe guinea pigs and rats, a boa constrictor, burrowing naked mole rats, and a bee colony. If you

EATS FOR KIDS When the tummies start rumbling, fill them up without leaving the museum. **Fountains Café** serves hot dogs, hamburgers, pizza, soup and sandwiches. Service is cafeteria-style, and prices start at under $2.

HEY KIDS! For many years, dinosaurs have been officially classified as reptiles, along with lizards and snakes. But now, many scientists believe these huge beasts may have been more like birds. Here are a two of the reasons why Dino may have been more like Tweety than Godzilla: Dinosaurs were warm-blooded and they had claws and feet like birds.

 200 Second Ave. N.

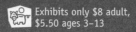 Exhibits only $8 adult,
$5.50 ages 3–13

206/443-2001; www.pacsci.org

Summer, daily 10 AM–6 PM;
School year, M–F 10 AM–5 PM,
Sa–Su 10 AM–6 PM

2 and up

have a bug-lover, the insect "petting" area will be a big hit. Kids can touch a variety of creepy-crawlies here, including a walking stick and a hissing cockroach.

At the Body Works exhibit, the focus is on the wonders of the human body. It's too advanced for kids under 7, but older children can check out their strength, hearing, eyesight, blood pressure, reaction time, and hand-eye coordination at various testing stations. Best of all, each station imparts a bit of knowledge about how the body works.

The Planetarium brings unearthly excitement to budding astronomers with 40-minute shows throughout the day. For the youngest visitors, the Just for Tots section is a kiddie paradise, complete with playhouse, water fun (not to worry, smocks are provided), tunnels, puppet theater, bubble wall, puzzles, and games. A nursing area with a comfy rocking chair and toys keeps older kids entertained while baby dines.

KEEP IN MIND Even though this is a kid-friendly place, a few areas are not designed for toddlers. Children must be at least 4 years old to attend the Planetarium shows. In the Tropical Butterfly House, strollers are not permitted because of the delicate insects flitting about the room and landing most anywhere, including the walkway. Toddlers should be carried to prevent a misstep that might spell disaster.

PIED PIPER PRESENTS

The Pied Piper of Hamelin had nothing on his namesake in Everett when it comes to the art of charming children. And the theater, a half-hour north of Seattle, doesn't even have to pull out a magic pipe to capture its youthful audiences' hearts.

Instead, it invites top-notch national and international performing groups to enchant audiences through entertaining performances. Pied Piper Presents is the children's program of Village Theatre, the resident troupe whose productions grace the stage at the Everett Performing Arts Center. The shows are picked to please a diverse audience of kids, and the theater's schedule helpfully recommends appropriate age groups for each performance.

Its programs, however, aren't limited to plays: magic shows, a popular international Christmas program, puppets, and dance troupes also share the stage. Most of the performances are just about right for the 6–10 age group, but some of the shows delight children as young as 3, and the typical 1-hour length is perfect for keeping the little ones' attention.

HEY KIDS! Being a performer on stage and wowing the audience looks like a lot of fun, doesn't it? But it's also a lot of hard work. Most actors spend years and years training, practicing, and working behind the scenes or playing small parts before they get a starring role. Is it worth it? Only if you really love what you're doing!

2710 Wetmore Ave., Everett

 $13 adults,
$11 under 18

 Oct–May, evenings and matinees

📞 425/257-6340;
www.piedpiperpresents.org

🚼 4 and up

There's also always a special production or two for teens, such as an American Indian dance montage.

In the summertime, Village Theatre puts its efforts into cultivating future performers. Auditions are held for two or three summer shows, including at least one student-run production and one professionally directed performance. For the latter, the tuition is about $300. The theater also hosts one- and two-week classes for aspiring actors. These programs cover an impressive variety of topics, ranging from stand-up comedy and choreography for older children, to fairytale-enactment for the younger set. The longer classes include mini-performances at the end. This program provides a wonderful, mind-opening summertime experience for kids, even if they don't have stars in their eyes.

EATS FOR KIDS
Petosa's (3121 Broadway, tel. 425/258–1544) serves a variety of fare, including great seafood, and has a good children's menu. If it's a pizza kind of night, check out **Romio's** (2803 Colby Ave., tel. 425/252–0800).

KEEP IN MIND The opening night gala in early October is an uproarious evening of clowns, jugglers, magicians, and kid-friendly treats—plus champagne and hors d'oeuvres for the grown-ups. Young party-goers who come dressed in costumes win special prizes. Although a big-splurge evening—$25 per person or $100 for a family—it's great fun and the proceeds provide scholarships to let low-income children in on the fun of enjoying a children's play.

PIKE PLACE MARKET

What would Seattle be without the Pike Place Market? Since 1907, people of all ages have flocked to the nation's oldest continuously operating farmers' market to be entertained by its outrageous colors, pungent aromas, and irrepressible spirit.

There's never a dull moment to be had in this famous downtown waterfront market. Street musicians and artists, often with dressed-up dogs in tow, add to the carnival atmosphere. Even 2-year-olds will giggle at the famous "flying fish" tossed about by the delightful fishmongers at Pike Place Fish. Look for the monkfish in the display case. If you look too closely, the staff will pull a hidden string to make it "snap" at you. It's best to advise younger kids that something fishy is in store. That way they'll be surprised and not scared.

HEY, KIDS

When you walk inside the market, the first thing you'll see is Rachel the pig. This giant bronze piggybank was modeled after a real 750-pound pig named Rachel. Go ahead and climb on her! She's also very useful. Rachel collects thousands of dollars every year to feed and care for needy people.

EATS FOR KIDS With cuisines ranging from Russian to Vietnamese, this is a great place to graze. Try the tasty chicken teriyaki/pineapple kabobs at **Mee Sum Pastry** (Pike Place Public Market, tel. 206/682–6780), across from the enclosed market. For a spontaneous picnic, buy a loaf of bread at **Le Panier Very French Bakery** (1902 Pike Place, tel. 206/441–3669), some fresh fruit and cheese from the stands, and take the family to Victor Steinbrueck Park on the waterfront. For dessert, try a mouthwatering chocolate croissant or fresh cinnamon roll from **Pike Place Bakery**, the market's original bakery, just inside the main Pike Street entrance.

 First and Pike Streets

 Free

206/587–0351;
www.pikeplacemarket.org

 M–Sa 9 AM–6 PM; Su 11AM–5 PM

All ages

If you're shopping for dinner, pick up some fresh local seafood and produce; many growers carry organic fruits and veggies. In the crafts area, at the south end of the market, check out the one-of-a-kind handmade items. With 250 shops and restaurants in and around the market, everyone is sure to find a favorite. For lots of kids, it's Wind-Up Toys, where you can try out the merchandise on the demo table. For once, you don't have to say: "Hands off!"

Older kids will enjoy the hour-long Heritage Tour, conducted Wednesday through Sunday, when guides take you through parts of the market you'd otherwise miss while explaining about its colorful past. The tour, which starts at 1531 Western Ave., costs $7 for adults and $5 for children under 18.

KEEP IN MIND Children love the market and tend to dash excitedly from stall to stall. But it gets very crowded, especially in the summertime, so keep them in sight. Strollers can be a challenge in the packed aisles, so allow for plenty of time. Restrooms are underground, but don't despair at the long flight of stairs! There's a ramp, though it's old and steep, further north. The waterfront area is generally safe, but expect a few panhandlers.

POINT DEFIANCE ZOO & AQUARIUM

This may not be the biggest zoo you've ever seen, but when it comes to variety and originality, Point Defiance doesn't monkey around.

You'll find elephants, monkeys, and leopards, but you'll also see lots of exotic residents, such as blind cave fish, poison dart frogs, and puffins. The staff enhances the experience by interacting with animals and guests alike. Kids as young as 2 love to watch the elephant eat apples, and inquisitive preschoolers are welcome to ask all the questions they want.

If your time is limited, head for the award-winning polar bear exhibit, one of the best in the world. These fierce predators resemble your toddler's cuddly teddy bears as they stretch their huge limbs, climb along the rocks, and paddle around in the pool. The other don't-miss spot is the aquarium section. A pair of smiley white Beluga whales delights even the youngest child by swimming up to the viewing windows. In the next tank, you'll find ET the walrus splashing around. When he arrived, he was was 2 months old. Now he's 19 years

HEY KIDS! A legend is a story that's been told for so many years, everyone thinks it's true. Sometimes it is; sometimes not. Legend has it that moray eels are vicious killers that attack humans. The truth is, they're very shy! They have sharp teeth to crush the shells of the animals they eat, and they breathe through their mouths. So when people see those mouths opening and closing, and all those teeth, they think the moray wants to attack. But unless you're a shellfish, the moray only bites if it thinks you might hurt it.

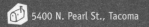
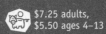

old, and a whopping 3,400 pounds! Be sure to visit the Giant Pacific, the largest octopus in the world, who can even open a jar to get at food.

Upstairs in the education room, young kids can work puzzles while older ones look through microscopes at sea stars and other creatures. The shark pool fascinates anyone over 6, and easy-to-read signs fill older kids in on the truth about these much-maligned creatures.

Reward the little ones for good behavior with a stop at the petting zoo. In addition to the common goats, pigs and ducks, you'll find some uncommon inhabitants such as peacocks, geese and pygmy goats. During the holidays, Point Defiance really shines with more than a half-million lights twinkling in the shapes of animals and nursery rhyme characters. It's guaranteed to brighten up any kid's day.

KEEP IN MIND This is a great zoo to visit if you have young children or kids of a wide age range. It's small enough that the tots won't have to be rushed along, but big enough to house a wide variety of animals that will keep any age group's attention.

EATS FOR KIDS

This is an idyllic place to have a picnic. You can munch away while you gaze at the Puget Sound. For dining in, try the park's **Red Rooster Grill,** next to the petting zoo, for sandwiches, hamburgers, salads, and snacks.

PORT GAMBLE HISTORIC MUSEUM

The Port Gamble Historic Museum, nestled behind the town's old General Store, tells the story of two friends, Andrew Jackson Pope and Frederic Talbot, who settled on Port Gamble in 1853 as the perfect spot for a sawmill to supply their San Francisco lumber business. To house their workers, they built a small town reminiscent of their native Maine.

Port Gamble is a real company town. A charming blend of Victorian gingerbread and Northeastern-style architecture set on a sparkling bay, the town was built and run for 140 years by the Pope and Talbot lumber company. The firm still owns the town, though the sawmill is long gone; its site is now leased out to a small wood-chipping business. Rumbling their way through town, huge trailers loaded with giant firs will fascinate big truck–loving kids.

Treasures celebrating this town's heritage, such as the huge 38-star U.S. flag that flew over the town from 1876–1890, fill the museum. The Heirlooms Room is packed with

GETTING THERE
Take the ferry from Seattle to Bainbridge Island, then drive along S.R. 305 North to S.R. 307 S. (Bond Rd). Turn right on Bond Rd. and drive 5 miles. Turn left onto Highway 104 West, at the sign to Port Gamble, then drive 3 miles and bear right.

KEEP IN MIND
If you have some extra time, stop in the Sea and Shore Museum, sprawled out on two floors above the Old General Store. Curator Tom Rice has assembled one of the largest shell collections in the country, and his magnificent display is free. More than 20,000 brilliantly colored shells of all shapes and sizes from sea creatures around the world fill dozens of delightfully mismatched showcases. There's no elevator, so leave the stroller in the General Store and carry the baby upstairs.

3 Rainier Ave., Port Gamble

 $2.50 adult;
free under 6

  May–Oct, daily 10:30–5;
Mar, Apr, Nov, by appointment only

 360/297–8074; www.ptgamble.com

8 and up

items from the town's 19th-century residents—clothes, pictures, tools, books, dishes, silver baby spoons—that show how similar their lives were to ours. Blasts from the past are provided via recreated scenes, including the elegant lobby of the Hotel Puget, once the bustling center of town. The 1903 establishment replaced an earlier hotel that provided gambling, drinking, billiards, and wild entertainment during an era when few mill workers had families.

You'll also see a replica of a cedar Indian house, Captain Talbot's cabin on the ship he sailed to Puget Sound, and an old-growth forest. Kids are always drawn to the old barbershop, with its customary red, white, and blue pole, and what looks like a medieval torture device. Not to worry, though; it was just an early model hair-curling machine. Stroller access is not a problem at the museum, but it's really designed with older kids in mind.

EATS FOR KIDS The **Old General Store** (1 Rainier Ave., tel. 360/297–7636) is not only historic, it's a fascinating place to explore. An old-fashioned ice cream cone is a great way to reward younger kids for their patience at the museum. The deli serves an assortment of soups, sandwiches, and pies. You can dine inside or outside on one of the benches overlooking the stunning blue bay.

REMLINGER FARMS

Give the kids a taste of rural life at this 200-acre farming fun center. Once just a roadside stand, it's not only a great spot to pick strawberries, raspberries, and pumpkins, but a sprawling family fun park with rides, ponies, and a petting zoo.

On the farm, you can watch the animals playing, sleeping, and eating in the barn. Then it's on to the fields. Picking berries is as much fun as it is educational, and tots can help out. The strawberries are ready to pick around mid-June; the raspberries in early July; and the pumpkins in October. A country store, open Mother's Day through Oct. 31, sells produce from Remlinger—including berries, jams, and their famous pies—and from farms all over Washington.

The Country Fair Family Fun Park is nonstop fun for the little ones. Pony rides, a miniature steam train, marionette shows that encourage audience participation, roller coasters, and other rides provide ample activities and entertainment for kids of all ages.

GETTING THERE The drive to Remlinger Farms, through rolling rural Washington, is about a 45-minute trip from Seattle. Take I-90 east from town to Exit 22, then follow the signs to Fall City. Once you're there, turn right at the only stop sign in town, cross the Snoqualmie River bridge, and take an immediate left onto Highway 203. Drive 5 more miles and you'll see the Remlinger Farms sign; turn right onto N.E. 32nd St., then proceed a quarter mile to the farm.

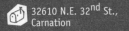 32610 N.E. 32nd St., Carnation

 425/333-4135

 $5 admission to Country Fair Family Fun Park

 Mother's Day–Jun., Sa–Su 11–5; July–Aug, daily, 11–5; Sept, Sa–Su 11–5

2 and up

Remlinger Farms also puts on special shows on the Fourth of July, Mother's Day, and Father's Day, which all involve special events or prices. The grand-slam event at Remlinger's is its annual Fall Harvest Festival, when the entire park turns orange with pumpkins and autumn leaves. There's a hay room for jumping, a haystack maze for exploring, haunted wagon rides, a not-so-scary house for tots, balloon twisting, and lots of extra activities. You can buy one of the scores of gourds on display throughout the grounds, or grab a wagon and head for the pumpkin patch to pick your own. At $9 per child and $8 per adult (babes-in-arms free), the fee scale seems a bit startling—until you get inside, where there's enough junior-size fun to last all day. This is one festival you have to see to believe.

KEEP IN MIND For a blast from the rural past, make a side trip to "downtown" Carnation, which has the feel of Mayberry. You won't see Andy Griffith patrolling the streets, but as you browse the little shops, it will seem like time has stood still.

EATS FOR KIDS Stop at the farm's comfortable **Country Kitchen Restaurant,** next to the market, for delicious, kid-friendly meals. While you're there, sample one of Remlinger's famous pies or pastries. You place your order at the counter, then take a seat. In Carnation, you can picnic at the **Tolt-MacDonald Park** or grab some tasty Chinese noodle dishes at **Ho Won** (31722 W. Eugene St., tel. 425/333–6288).

ROSALIE WHYEL MUSEUM OF DOLL ART

Anyone who's ever loved a doll will find something to tug at their heartstrings at this unusual museum. The award-winning Rosalie Whyel is a fantasyland of miniature Victorian houses and dolls from every corner of the world.

Only two-thirds of Whyel's collection of 3,000 figures is shown at one time. Video kiosks scattered throughout the facility provide facts about the art and history of dollmaking. You'll find toddlers and teenagers sharing the benches in front of the monitors, glued to the show. The museum's collection is arranged through thoughtful and educational groupings. As you wander through the rooms, the history of dollmaking unfolds, country by country and era by era—from a high-society English lady, handcrafted in 1680, to a mass-produced Bart Simpson. One exhibit worth pointing out to older children is the non-native display, which shows the difference between dolls made by artists within a culture and those made to represent that culture by another region, such as Indian, Chinese,

KEEP IN MIND Girls as young as 2 will squeal their way through the two floors of displays at the doll museum. Their brothers may require some coaxing, but once inside, most boys under 9 will enjoy the action figures, mechanical displays, and even the incredibly detailed dollhouses. Just don't ask them to admit it!

HEY KIDS! It's hard to imagine, but baby dolls once never existed. Until the middle of the 19th century, dolls just looked like small adults. But in the 1860s, some French artists decided to make dolls that were chubby and cute, with big eyes and heads. They dressed their baby dolls in beautiful handmade clothing, and children fell in love. But they had to play gently, because these dolls had breakable heads. Baby dolls are not as fragile today, but they're loved as much as ever.

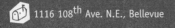
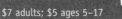

and African dolls created by Europeans. The differences in facial characteristics and dress are a fascinating lesson in perspective.

A variety of elaborate, handmade dollhouses displayed throughout the museum are guaranteed to elicit oohs and ahs from kids of all ages. You can even try to lure them away to view the old-fashioned child's room with its charming mechanical displays, including a circling train, rocking chair, and rocking horse. This is every kid's dream room. And yes, Mom, you'll find a first-edition Barbie. She's downstairs in the 20th Century Dolls room, next to all her pals. Go ahead, dig out your old Color 'n' Curl set tonight after the kids go to bed.

Need a place for a special occasion? You can rent out the doll museum's meeting area for a party. This sunny room opens onto a patio and costs $50 an hour. The museum can provide you with a list of caterers to serve your partyers' favorite treats.

EATS FOR KIDS Just two blocks away, **Red Robin** (11021 N.E. 8th St., tel. 425/453–9522) serves meals and sandwiches with younger diners in mind, and a cheerful staff carries crayons for drawing. If you have a little grazer, head for the buffet at **Zoopa** (1070 Bellevue Square, tel. 425/453–7887) inside the Bellevue Square Mall. You'll find oodles of soups, salads, pastas, and pizza.

SEATTLE AQUARIUM

The magic and mystery of undersea life unfolds in dazzling detail at Seattle Aquarium. Even infants enjoy the facility's vast collection of mostly Northwest sea life, ranging from the leafy sea dragons, which look like globs of floating seaweed, to an enormous, 650-volt electric eel.

The displays are made even more fun and educational with hands-on exhibits geared toward kids as young as 2. The Giant Pacific Octopus is fascinating enough on its own, but the museum puts icing on the cake. Older kids can read lots of fun facts about these surprisingly shy creatures, such as how smart they are and how quickly they can change color to hide in a new spot.

At the Pacific Coral Reef, children can identify dozens of colorful creatures inside the tanks with the help of charts on the wall. Feeding times are wildly popular with the younger elementary set. Schedules at the entrance tell you when the diving birds, coral reef animals,

HEY KIDS! One of the most fascinating fish at the aquarium is the seahorse, which is not a horse at all, even though it looks like a tiny horse without legs. Seahorses are different from other fish in many ways. For example, the mother lays her eggs inside the father's pouch. He carries the growing babies for 6 weeks, then releases them into the water. How many do you think a father seahorse can fit into his tiny pouch? The record was 1,572 babies!

otters, and sharks eat their dinner. The Discovery Lab is another great stop, with its tanks of clams, anemones, and other sea creatures available for touching. In the otter section, kids can make crayon "rubbings" of otter footprints. The can also look inside a refrigerator stocked with the massive amount of food they'd have to eat every day to consume as much as an otter.

Even for the 2- to 6-year-old, endless options abound. The huge felt board "aquarium," with its myriad felt sea creatures, reinforces what they've seen in the tanks. In the Marsh Room, little ones can drape themselves in terrycloth costumes and, *voila!*, they become ducks, ladybugs or whales, waddling, crawling or swimming through a log tunnel into a spongy "marsh." The only touch that's missing is a mirror for checking out their new look.

EATS FOR KIDS
At the end of Pier 59, you can munch on clams and fish at **Steamer's Seafood** (1500 Alaskan Way, tel. 206/624–0312). If you're feeling too emotionally connected to the sea, cross the street and dine at **Godfather's Pizza** (1414 Alaskan Way, tel. 206/ 621–7835).

KEEP IN MIND If your kids just can't get enough of the undersea world, their adventures don't have to stop at the exhibits. Special programs designed for all age groups include the Family Hour offered at three levels, starting at the under-3 age group. This three-day series includes puppets, songs, art projects, and live-animal visits. The program costs about $30 for an adult/child pair, and $15 per additional child. One-day classes are also available for about half the price.

SEATTLE ART MUSEUM

Can't imagine your kids begging to stay just a little longer at an art museum? Wait till you check out SAM's "Please Touch" room, tucked away behind the Near Eastern exhibit on the third floor. This spot brings art to life for children, stimulating them to put those active imaginations to use.

One wall is stacked with bins of fabulous stuff for make-believe sessions. Kids can try on the historic costumes, play with puppets, twine their own straw mats, host a Japanese "tea party," and make construction-paper baskets. They can even put on plays or puppet shows on a stage. Older children can browse through the books or pop an art history video into the TV while their younger siblings play.

SAM's kid appeal goes beyond the activity room. Consider saving this room for last; seeing the art exhibits first will inspire their role-playing. Don't miss the Northwest display on the fourth floor. This collection of colorful Native American objects shows off the artistry

KEEP IN MIND Special exhibits are often accompanied by an "artist's studio," where you'll find smocks, easels, paints, chalk, hats, costumes, and even live models like the artist used. It's enough to turn your child into a budding *artiste!*

HEY KIDS! Say hello to the big man who greets you outside the museum. He's 48 feet tall, made of black steel, and he pounds his hammer twice a minute, 15 hours a day. No wonder he looks a little tired! The Hammering Man is only 7 inches thick, so he's sometimes called "the flat man." When a crane lifted him in 1991 to be placed outside the museum, he tumbled to the ground, digging holes in the pavement. It took a year to fix him, and he's been hammering ever since—except on Labor Day, when he takes the day off.

 100 University St.

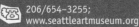 206/654-3255;
www.seattleartmuseum.org

 Over age 13, $7

T–Su 10–5; Th 10–9

4 and up

of local Northwest tribes. Colorful totem poles, ornate ceremonial robes, bear and eagle war helmets, and elaborate raven masks fill the collection. Explain to your kids that dancers acting out the tribes' traditional tales used these huge masks.

Other child-pleasers at SAM include the African exhibit, with its beaded headdresses; the Japanese display, with its exotic robes, kimonos and screens; and the life-size camels and rams on the landings of the Grand Staircase. No rides on these beasts, though; they've been retired since the ancient Ming Dynasty.

SAM has limited but impressive collections of art from still more lands and eras, but you'll have to decide, based on your children's ages and personalities, how many to see. For kids under 7, three or four exhibits should be enough. Don't forget that admission to the museum, a few blocks south of Pike Place Market, is free the first Thursday of every month.

EATS FOR KIDS The museum **café** serves a variety of food that's tasty and affordable. If the line's too long, walk across the street to **Wolfgang Puck Cafe** (1225 1st, tel. 206/621–9653) for wood-fired pizzas. While waiting for the food, check out the whimsical, colorful art on the walls and counters all around you.

SEATTLE CENTER HOUSE

On one of those wet Seattle days, head to the Seattle Center House, near the Space Needle, where it's cozy and dry and you never know what's going on: a local children's choir or a group of European folk dancers. The whole family will be tapping their toes, and the uninhibited under-6'ers can sashay on the roomy sidelines. No need to keep little fidgeters still.

Between performances, the kiddie toys come out on the dance floor—plastic cars, trikes, and wagons that widen the eyes of the 2–6 set. The frequent art bazaars introduce kids to a bit of culture. If the kids still have energy to burn, head upstairs to the Children's Room, where tots can climb, crawl, slide, and read to their hearts'—and their parents'—content. For easy stroller access, look for the glass elevator in the food court, near the east end of the building. While you keep your toddler company, you can also keep an eye on older siblings through the glass walls of the Children's Room. A play area just

HEY KIDS! The Seattle Center House is a favorite gathering place for people from all over the world. More than 100 years ago, the same spot was a popular gathering place for Native American tribes who came together for huge feasts called potlatches. The after-dinner entertainment was spectacular, featuring ceremonial dancing with beautiful robes and large wooden masks. The dancers acted out the tribes' traditional stories about the Earth and the heavens.

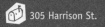 305 Harrison St.

206/684-7200

 Activities priced separately; discount passes available

 Su–Th 11–6; F–Sa 11–8

1 and up

outside the tot room keeps children ages 4 to 8 amused with a chalkboard, gazebo, giant abacus, and larger slide.

If it's a nice day, head outside the Center House to the Fun Forest Amusement Park. It's a perpetual carnival, with rides for every age group, from a carousel to a mini-train to a Ferris wheel. And if you need to dodge a few drops, duck inside the pavilion, where you'll find more rides, along with an assortment of arcade games, laser tag, and Seattle-themed putt-putt golf.

On warm days, the elaborate fountain just outside the Seattle Center House draws local kids by the dozen. You'll see them in their bathing suits, frolicking in the spray for hours while their parents soak up the rays on the adjacent grassy hillside. It's a great place for a picnic, too!

EATS FOR KIDS
More than 18 kid-friendly restaurants line the Seattle Center House. You can enjoy an Italian dinner at **Michelangelo's Bistro & Bar** (305 Harrison St., tel. 206/441–6600). At **Café Beignet** (305 Harrison St., tel. 206/441–0262) you can indulge in the tasty New Orleans–style namesakes, which are made to order and dusted with powdered sugar.

KEEP IN MIND You can hop on the monorail for a scenic ride from Seattle Center to downtown and back. It goes right through the guitar-shaped Experience Music Project (see #56). A round-trip ticket costs $2.50 for adults and $1 for ages 6–11. The monorail goes downtown, stopping outside the top floor of Westlake Center Mall. If you want to explore downtown, you'll find a well-hidden elevator to the far left as you face Westlake.

SEATTLE CHILDREN'S THEATRE

It's all about kids at this theater, one of the finest playhouses of its kind in the country. With its colorful sets, elaborate costumes, and professional actors, the SCT keeps its youthful audiences enthralled.

The SCT entertains about 300,000 guests during its six-play regular season, mixing things up with a selection of beloved classics and world-premiere contemporary plays. Plays aimed at the youngest theater-goers, like *Winnie the Pooh,* are alternated with performances for elementary-age children, like *The Red Balloon*. A few more sophisticated stories like *Animal Farm* are thrown in for teen appeal.

The SCT plays aimed at the youngest kids are shorter, about 1 hour, and audience participation is invited. Intermission comes at just the right time for little ones to run off some steam and grab a snack. The youngest recommended age is 4, but 3-year-olds with good attention spans will also sit spellbound.

HEY KIDS! Why not put on your very own play? Pick out a book and a favorite character, then ask an adult to help you make a costume. Nothing fancy; just use your imagination. A bathrobe makes a perfect cape. A towel works as a magic carpet. And a few crayons, some tape, and scissors can turn a grocery bag into a crown. Practice your scene in your room, then act it out for Mom or Dad. Don't forget to take a bow!

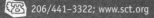
Two auditoriums, the 500-seat Charlotte Martin and the 300-seat Eve Alvord, handle its often-overlapping schedules. The theater is at the Seattle Center complex, west of the Space Needle. Be sure to reserve your seats early, as tickets sell out quickly. The regular season runs September through June.

In July and August, the staff keeps busy with workshops for children ages 3 to 19. These are held in a technical pavilion that houses prop, costume, and scene shops as well as rehearsal rooms. Older youths with a serious interest in theater can spend their summers studying acting, voice, dance, and scenery preparation. Workshop participants put on performances at the end of the summer. Children especially enjoy watching actors their own age take the stage. By the time the curtain falls, your little theater-goer may have caught the acting bug, too.

EATS FOR KIDS When you reserve your seat, ask for a sack lunch. They're reasonably priced and nutritious, with names like the Pooh & Tigger turkey sandwich and the Mrs. Piggle Wiggle PB&J. They'll be waiting on a table, marked with your name, when you arrive at the theater. Eat them right away, or during intermission. If you want to eat after the show, try the **The Magic Dragon** (305 Harrison St., tel. 206/443–0728), in the Seattle Center, for a variety of tasty noodle dishes.

SEATTLE IMAX DOME THEATER

What kid hasn't created some semblance of a "volcano" on the kitchen table at one time or another? You can show yours a real one—minus the messy lava and ash—at *The Eruption of Mount St. Helens,* the feature film at Seattle's IMAX. The kids will sit spellbound as the magnificent mountain blows its top right before their eyes. Dramatic before-and-after pictures stretch out before—and above—you in this 40-minute film. It's the main attraction at the domed theater, perched on a pier along the downtown waterfront.

Youngsters will be fascinated, and adults humbled, by the power of the volcano, which spewed out enough ash one fateful day in 1980 to cover the city of Seattle to the top of the Space Needle. Fortunately for Seattle, the plume of ash blew east. The movie, which was nominated for an Academy Award in 1980, has been updated to show the long-term effects of the volcano. The fish are still gone from Spirit Lake, and signs of life are just returning to miles of forest flattened like Lincoln Logs.

KEEP IN MIND Reward your kids for sitting still at the IMAX by walking next door to Waterfront Park after the show. You won't find any grass here, but wide platforms overlooking Puget Sound allow for plenty of room to stretch little legs. Be sure to peer through the telescopes at the islands across the bay. On the other side of the park, Pier 57 houses a fun room with pinball, air hockey, and video games. Kids can ride the carousel for a dollar.

 Pier 59, Seattle waterfront

 $7 adult; $6 ages 6–18

 Daily; times vary

206/622–1868

4 and up

When you enter the theater, you'll have to leave your stroller in the lobby. The script is simple enough for most 6-year-olds to get the idea. If not, the pictures sum things up. A word of warning: The noise and devastation, which feels lifelike in the IMAX auditorium, may frighten very young or sensitive kids.

The Mount St. Helens film is the only permanent movie at the theater. But if volcanic eruptions leave you cold, you can choose from several other IMAX films, which typically showcase interesting regions and animals from around the globe. You can see a second film the same day for $2 more.

EATS FOR KIDS
At the sidewalk end of Pier 59, you'll find a **Steamer's Seafood** stand with tasty food and a kids' menu. At Pier 57, you can dine inside at **The Crab Pot** (tel. 206/624–1890) on burgers and sandwiches; the kids' menu is sure to please.

HEY, KIDS! Think Mount St. Helens has been tamed? Think again! Deep inside the mountain, the volcanic cone is slowly rebuilding itself. In 200 years, it will be as high as ever! Does that mean it will erupt in 200 years? No one knows for sure. Scientists call Mount St. Helens a ticking time bomb, which means it could blow its stack tomorrow—or in 100 years. Fortunately, scientists now have better tools to warn us when a volcano is ready to erupt.

SEATTLE HARBOR CRUISE

Seattle's harbor is not just for show—it's an honest-to-gosh working port. On this hour-long cruise, you'll find out just how busy it is. As a bonus, a great view of the city skyline unfolds. If you have younger kids, arrive early, stake out a table downstairs, and spread out those toys and books. Later, you can go upstairs and take a walk around the deck.

Your guide points out interesting landmarks as you float along such as the Edgewater Hotel, which became famous when the Beatles stayed there and fished from their window, and ritzy Queen Anne Hill, where the TV character Frasier makes his home. On a clear day, you'll also get a great view of spectacular Mount Rainier and possibly Mount Olympus, the largest mountain in the Olympic chain. As you pass the towering Space Needle, you'll be told that Puget Sound is deep enough to swallow the whole thing.

EATS FOR KIDS The **snack bar** on the ship serves mainly chips, soft drinks, and other munchies, so you may want to pack a picnic lunch. You can eat on the boat or a waterfront bench. For terrific seafood, try **Elliott's Oyster House** (Pier 56, tel. 206/623–4340).

HEY KIDS! As you probably know, it rains and rains and rains in Seattle. Why is it so wet? When you're out on the boat, you'll see mountains on both sides of the city—the Olympics to the west and the Cascades to the east. Seattle lies in a valley in between. So when a storm moves in, it gets trapped between the mountains, right over the city. It just keeps raining on Seattle until the clouds run out of water. So carry an umbrella!

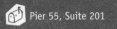 Pier 55, Suite 201

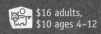 $16 adults,
$10 ages 4–12

 206/623–4252

 Daily; departures vary seasonally

4 and up

Then it's on to the business side of the harbor: the port where grain is loaded from huge silos onto ships on sunny days and the buildings that store those famous Washington apples before they are shipped to other ports. You'll pass the city fishing pier, made of recycled materials in true Northwest style, and the boat-maintenance area, a highlight for young mariners. On a typical day, boats pull up to the refueling pier; huge container ships are loaded and unloaded with giant orange cranes; and freight ships wait in dry dock for painting or repairs. Many of the ships have traveled from as far away as Asia.

If you bring tiny tots along, they'll have lots of room to run on the large carpeted area in front of the snack stand. They can also walk up and down the stairs and around the upper deck. Hang onto them as you leave the boat, though—they might be kind of wobbly till they get their "land legs" back again!

KEEP IN MIND Argosy Cruises leads a variety of outings in addition to the basic Harbor Cruise. The two-hour Lake Cruise explores Lake Washington; the 2-hour Locks Cruise takes you through the Hiram Chittendon Locks and the Ship Canal; and the Royal Argosy goes on lunch and dinner cruises, with food prepared by a talented local chef.

SEATTLE METROPOLITAN POLICE MUSEUM

At this unusual museum in the historic Pioneer Square district, they really mean business when it comes to playing cops and robbers. Of course, the emphasis is on the good-guy role. Watch your little law enforcer's eyes light up when he or she spots the boxes of badges, handcuffs, bullet-proof vests, and helmets—all authentic equipment from local police agencies. Add a Seattle Police or King County deputy's shirt and the fun begins.

Above a big mirror sits a red-and-blue police car light, which the kids can turn on with a switch. Mom and Dad, can you say "photo op"? Got any dastardly villains in your family? They can be "locked up" in the jail cell around the corner. The kids can take turns trying out the handcuffs.

Children up to 10 can also try out an authentic—if out-of-date—emergency 911 dispatch system. They can sit at the controls, grab the radio, and push buttons to their hearts' content. Lending a touch of authenticity, a police scanner broadcasts real Seattle Police radio

HEY KIDS! Every town in America has police officers to keep the citizens safe. But that wasn't always the case. Before the early 1800s, voluntary night watchmen or military soldiers patrolled the streets. The idea of hiring police officers and giving them uniforms started in London, England. The officers are called "bobbies," after Sir Robert Peel, the man who came up with the plan.

 317 Third Ave. South

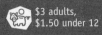 $3 adults, $1.50 under 12

T–Sa 11–4

206/748–9991

5 and up

communications in the background. If you have just one child, try to bring a friend along to make the role-playing that much more fun.

Children with an interest in law enforcement can check out the educational exhibits, which tell how police departments began and how they've evolved over the years. The museum has a terrific collection of police items, many of them donated by current and retired officers. Kids can see how uniforms, badges, handcuffs, billy clubs and other equipment have changed over the years.

Also displayed are rare original FBI "Wanted" posters from the 1930s gangster era. A poster of John Dillinger bears an officer's red-penciled notation: "Rubbed out." Even though the museum's focus is toeing the line, you'll find the staff very kid-tolerant. It would be a crime to miss it!

KEEP IN MIND
The museum is compact enough for parents and older kids to enjoy most of the displays before the little ones get too fidgety. However, if your kids get restless, especially those under 8, stop at the play area halfway through the museum for a little respite.

EATS FOR KIDS Stroll down to the **Elliott Bay Café** (1st Ave. S., tel. 206/682–6664), in the basement of the historic Elliott Bay Book Company. The menu is particularly kid-pleasing: sandwiches include peanut butter-and-banana and turkey-and-cranberry. Wolf them down there or take them to the **Waterfall Gardens** (219 2nd Ave. S.), where you can sit on benches and listen to the crashing falls.

SEATTLE SYMPHONY/ BENAROYA HALL

W ho says the symphony is just for grown-ups? Certainly not the Seattle Symphony, though it performs at the elegant, sophisticated Benaroya Hall, known for its glamour and those breathtaking chandeliers by famed glassmaker Dale Chihuly. When the symphony is performing for children, all those grand airs are set aside.

The Tiny Tots series keeps kids clapping, singing, and swaying to the music on Tuesday and Saturday mornings, about every other month. Children up to age 4 are welcome, but the 2-year-old and up audience will appreciate it most. Small ensembles of symphony players share the stage with young musicians and performers who get the kids involved in songs, stories, and games. Admission is $5 per person.

Five- to 12-year-olds graduate into Discover Music, a concert series tailored just for them. The five-concert schedule runs October through June and provides a taste of "real" symphony music, presented in a way that won't intimidate. The kids are introduced to various

EATS FOR KIDS

Gretchen's, a sandwich bar inside Benaroya Hall, serves a variety of lunch items at affordable prices. Across the street, try **Quizno's Classic Subs** (1401 2nd St., tel. 206/652–8427).

HEY KIDS! The Seattle Symphony has a long history. It started in 1903 when 24 musicians got together and formed an orchestra. By 1924, the symphony had grown to 90 players, and their conductor was Madame Davenport Engberg, the first woman to conduct a symphony. She hired both men and women, even though back then, women were rarely seen on the symphony stage. Today, it doesn't matter who you are, only how well you play.

cultures and classical composers through fables, stories, and sing-a-longs. Mimes and actors often share the stage with the full symphony orchestra. The cost is $17 for adults and $11 for ages 5–12. For secondary-school students, the "Meet the Beat" morning concert series takes them on lively symphonic tours around the globe. One program features salsa music and a limbo contest. The cost is $8 per person.

High school music students are also invited to attend symphony rehearsals, where they are encouraged to ask questions during the breaks. Older children are also welcome at the pre-concert lectures hosted by composers, musicians, and conductors an hour before many of the symphony's performances.

Anyone who knows kids knows the natural connection between children and music. The Seattle Symphony aims to raise that musical bar a bit above the Hokey Pokey.

KEEP IN MIND At the interactive Soundbridge Seattle Symphony Music Discovery Center, best appreciated by kids age 4 and up, kids can touch and play musical instruments, visit a listening bar to sample symphonic tunes, or watch a virtual conducting experience. A favorite exhibit shows kids how symphonic music plays out in their daily lives, from TV commercials to movies. The museum (tel. 206/336–6600) is open 10 AM–6 PM, Tuesday through Sunday. It costs $7 for adults and $5 for ages 4 and up.

SCENIC TOURS & FLIGHTS

For a real eagle's eye view of the Emerald City and its natural surroundings, hop onto the amiable George Kirkish's Alaskan bush plane for a trip your family won't soon forget.

The 20-minute flight, the Downtown Seattle, gives you a great overview of the city. Kirkish whisks you above the skyscrapers and over the towering Space Needle, along the tranquil Puget Sound and the busy Ballard Locks, then past the elegant mansions along Lake Washington, including Bill Gates' home. The plane holds three people; however, a baby or tot can ride on your lap for free.

For kids under 6, this is the best flight to choose. Depending on your little aviator's age and interest level, you might opt for one of Kirkish's more elaborate trips for an older child. The pre-packaged flights last up to four hours, and you can also custom-tailor a trip if you like. For $186, you can take a flight that's double the length of the basic trip

HEY KIDS! How long have people wanted to fly? Probably ever since the first human being saw a bird soaring through the sky. But it was just a dream until Dec. 17, 1903, when brothers Orville and Wilbur Wright took the first airplane flight at Kitty Hawk, N.C. To get their plane into the air, both brothers had to lie down, twist their hips around and turn the rudder handle. It was a lot of work, but they liked it so much, they flew it four times that same day.

 7149 Perimeter Rd.,
Boeing Field

 Starts at $126

 By appointment

877/475-3247

2 and up

and adds a foray into the hidden bays and inlets of several magical islands. Another flight circles Mount Rainier, providing a glimpse of spectacular ice caves, glaciers, and waterfalls—and in the distance, you can see Mount St. Helens. This hour-long expedition costs $246. Add another hundred bucks and you can continue on the Oregon, to peer inside the eye of the still-active volcano.

Another option takes you up over the idyllic San Juan Islands, where you'll encounter leaping orca whales on almost every flight during the summer migration. Even though it's 90 minutes long, the search for sea life keeps kids interested. At $396, however, it will take a bite out of your budget. A scenic flight of the area can get pretty pricey, but if this is a big-splurge item for you, you won't find a better way to wing your way across this incredibly diverse area.

EATS FOR KIDS
There aren't many places to eat near Boeing Field; the closest is **Alki Bakery** (5700 1st St., tel. 206/762–5700). This landmark Seattle lunch spot serves an overwhelming variety of salads and sandwiches. You might even be tempted to skip lunch and go straight for a homemade dessert.

KEEP IN MIND Reserve as much in advance as possible for a flight. Kirkish's scenic flights are popular, and in between he teaches aviation students, so his schedule can get pretty booked. Kirkish flies out of the Galvin Executive Terminal at Boeing Field, 10 minutes south of downtown Seattle, but he can arrange to pick you up at any Puget Sound airport.

SKAGIT COUNTY HISTORICAL MUSEUM

The sleepy town of La Conner is a bit of a hike from Seattle, but its spectacular scenery and friendly people make the drive worth it. And this historical museum is the icing on the cake. It focuses on the people who shaped the land and the way they lived their lives. Everything you see on display was owned and used by local residents.

The story starts with the Native Americans. Encourage older children to imagine how these people lived, using their cleverly fashioned tools, baskets, and canoes. Kids will discover how the Europeans later influenced the area by bringing new technologies such as plows and stump-pullers, and new industries such as mining and logging. A replica of an old general store, complete with food bins, mailboxes, fruit, and a scale, shows how the settlers shopped. A map from 1894 shows how Skagit County looked at the time.

HEY KIDS!
Life used to be a lot harder than it is today. People had to make their own soap, grow their own food, wash their clothes by hand, and cook over a fire. Kids were expected to pitch in and help with all the chores, too.

KEEP IN MIND Each spring, the area shows off its glorious blanket of flowers during the famous Skagit Valley Tulip Festival (tel. 360/428–5959). Settled by tulip growers from Holland, Skagit is one of the nation's top tulip producers. Visitors can pick up a "tulip map" at the visitor center and stop by dozens of colorful fields. There are also art shows and barbecues. Festival dates vary each year, but it is usually held in April and lasts about three weeks.

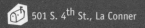
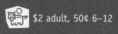

Local industries are highlighted, from mining to fishing to farming. Point out how much harder folks had to work 100 years ago to do things now handled by machines. The old farm tool display will help illustrate your point. The stump puller, for example, pulled stumps from the ground, with one end attached to a stump and the other end to a horse. The horse would walk around in a circle until the rope grew tense enough to pull out the stump. The collection of antique buggies and cars includes a 1913 Surrey and a 1923 Model T.

You'll find plenty of room for strollers here, but few exhibits will interest children under 5. They'll enjoy the display of old dolls and teddy bears, but these items cannot be handled. That's hard to explain to a little one. For everyone else, this museum is a wonderful window into the past.

EATS FOR KIDS Drive into downtown La Conner, where the little shops and galleries beckon. A fun place to eat lunch is **The Next Chapter** (721 S. 1st St., tel. 360/466–2665), which is a combination bookstore and café serving soups and sandwiches. **Whiskers Café** (128 S. 1st St., tel. 360/466–1008) serves tasty fish and chips, burgers, cookies, and ice cream.

SNOQUALMIE FALLS

F ew major cities have a wilderness wonderland just a half-hour away, and few cherish it more than the nature-loving Seattleites. Snoqualmie Falls was a sacred spot to the Snoqualmie and other Northwest tribes, and when you see it, you'll understand why. The falls cascade 270 feet down a rocky cliff, crashing with graceful splendor into the river below. That's 100 feet farther than Niagara Falls.

The thundering water and the enormous splash as it hits the river transfixes even infants. Decks with railings at the top of the cliff provide excellent views. Walk down to the hiking area, where a huge meadow beckons for romping and picnicking. Chirping birds and colorful flowers will light up the eyes of the youngest children. The main hiking trail takes you all the way to the bottom of the gorge, where the falls meet the river. But that may be too far for children under 8 to walk. Even if yours are older, remember that the return trip is

EATS FOR KIDS Perched at the top of the falls is **The Attic** (6501 Railroad Ave., tel. 425/888–2556), upstairs in the luxurious Salish Lodge & Spa. It's more casual than the lodge's main restaurant and has a heart-stopping view of the falls. If you want the complete outdoor experience, pack a lunch and enjoy it in the meadow.

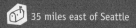 35 miles east of Seattle

 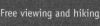 Free viewing and hiking

 Dawn until dusk

425/888–2556 Salish Lodge;
425/888–3030 Northwest Railway

1 and up

uphill! Though the view at the bottom is spectacular, you needn't go all the way down to enjoy the tranquil streams, ancient cedars, and wildlife.

If you have time, chug through the scenic Snoqualmie Valley on a restored steam train, which runs on weekends from April through October. In December, a special Santa Train runs, but be sure to reserve a spot well in advance. These tracks once carried lumber and potatoes out of the valley, but were eventually abandoned in favor of trucks and highways. The original station has been restored and turned into a museum, where you can also catch the train. The Northwest Railway Museum (tel. 425/888–3030) is just down the road from the falls, at 38625 S.E. King St., across from Railroad Avenue. The 5-mile ride is just the right length to keep the fun on track for even the littlest engineers.

GETTING THERE
To get to Snoqualmie Falls, head east from Seattle on I–90. Take Exit 25, then turn left onto Snoqualmie Parkway. Turn left again at Railroad Avenue, and the falls are a quarter-mile on the left.

HEY KIDS! The road from Seattle to Snoqualmie is Interstate 90. But long before it was paved, this road was a Native American trail. The Snoqualmie tribes traveled this route to get to the huge waterfall, where they gathered to trade goods and hold tribal meetings.

SPACE NEEDLE

If you have a budding astronaut in your family, you can blast off into the clouds together without ever leaving downtown Seattle. Just hop onto the Space Needle elevator for an exciting ride that sends you soaring 520 feet above the sidewalks. Don't forget to admire the beautiful Emerald City on your way up!

The elevator is almost always packed, so position shorter kids toward the front and sides for the best view. After "lift-off," glass walls will reveal Seattle in its entire splendor. If you have riders who are a little nervous about heights, have them stand toward the back and enjoy the elevator operator's silly jokes. By the time the giggling stops—just 43 seconds after departure—you've reached the observation deck.

The kids can roam to their hearts' content on the glass-surrounded promenade. Toddlers love racing around the deck, so you'll want to keep a close eye on them. They can't

HEY, KIDS!

You're not the only ones who doodle on your place mats! The man who dreamed up the Space Needle, Edward E. Carlson, made his first drawing of the futuristic tower on a place mat at a coffee shop. Two years later, he got to see his vision rise into reality. Doodling sometimes pays off!

KEEP IN MIND For a real treat, take the family all the way up to the revolving Sky City restaurant, near the top of the Needle. Kids love spinning around (slowly!) while they eat, and adults marvel at the stunning, 360-degree panoramic view of Seattle. Take the kids at lunchtime to save a few bucks. Your meal includes a trip to the observation deck, so no need to buy separate tickets. Children are welcome at any time, and your server will probably suggest finishing up with the kid-pleasing Lunar Orbiter ice cream, served in swirls of dry-ice Seattle "fog."

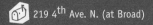 219 4th Ave. N. (at Broad)

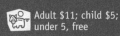 Adult $11; child $5; under 5, free

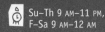 Su–Th 9 AM–11 PM, F–Sa 9 AM–12 AM

800/937-9582; www.spaceneedle.com

 2 and up

fall off, but they can get lost in the summertime crowds. Kids can peek through the free telescopes for an even better view of the area. Informational signs tell you what to look for in each direction. "Assign" your kids to spot these sights: the carousel and Ferris wheel below the Needle; the snow-capped Cascade Mountains to the east; and the sparkling blue Puget Sound, dotted with ferry boats, to the west. On a clear day, you can also see Mount Rainier looming ghostlike to the south.

The Space Needle holds a special place in Seattle's heart. It was built as the centerpiece for the 1962 World's Fair and painted, appropriately, a shade called Astronaut White. For the Needle's 40th birthday, the city spent $20 million on fresh paint and a facelift. Back in 1962, it only cost $4.5 million to build the whole thing!

EATS FOR KIDS For something more down to earth, head next door to **Seattle Center House** (305 Harrison St., tel. 206/684-7200), where you'll find a mecca of child-oriented dining spots arranged around a large, airy room. Your kids can even eat at a tot-size table next to yours. Try **Steamer's Seafood Café** for fish 'n' chips (305 Harrison St., tel. 206/728-2228) or the ever-popular **The Frankfurter** (305 Harrison St., tel. 206/728-7243) for dogs served your favorite way.

STONE GARDENS

I f your kids are climbing the walls, you may as well let them do it here. You and your family can spend a whole day "bouldering," or free-climbing, around a huge indoor gravel pit. The textured walls are sloped and angled at varying degrees of difficulty, and dotted with multicolored fiberglass "rocks" in all shapes and sizes.

Each section is labeled to tell you its level of physical challenge. Beginners can grab whichever rocks are convenient and climb away. Don't let kids plant their toes any higher than their height plus an outstretched arm. More experienced climbers clamber along the walls following paths marked with colored tabs. Even toddlers have been seen scrambling up the walls here, but don't try it unless your little spider is unusually strong.

For most kids, the rope section is more fun than the bouldering area, but the extra excitement comes at a price. The cost includes climbing shoes (you can just wear your

KEEP IN MIND From 5–7 PM Monday and Friday, and 10 AM–noon Saturday, Stone Gardens holds its Kids Climb program for children ages 6–16. At $25, it's a better bargain than the regular $24 hourly rate. Kids won't get their own attendant, but the four-to-one student/instructor ratio ensures a good amount of personal attention. Call ahead to register. The facility also holds climbing camps in the summertime for youngsters as young as 5, with both indoor and outdoor climbs.

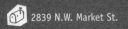 2839 N.W. Market St.

206/781-9828

 Bouldering, $12/day adult, $10/day 17 & under; one-on-one rope-climbing, $24/hour

M, W, F, Sa, 10–10; T, Th 6 AM–11 PM; Su 10–7

6 and up

sneakers to boulder) and an attendant to give advice and hold the ropes. For rope-climbing, kids are strapped into harnesses with ropes that attach to the ceiling. An attendant pulls on the end of the rope and calls out suggestions for finger- and toeholds. Youngsters who do well on the easiest slope can move on to harder ones until their hour is up. Parents can stand below and watch, or go up on the catwalk and snap pictures.

If you've never been in a rock-climbing gym, this is a whole new world, one that looks sort of like an upside-down desert. People of all ages and skill levels crawl spiderlike across the 40-foot-tall adobe-colored walls, many of them in training for the real peaks of the Northwest. And who knows? You might just get inspired to tackle Mt. Rainier yourself after your day at Stone Gardens. At the very least, everyone is guaranteed a good night's sleep.

HEY KIDS! With such well-known peaks as 14,000-foot tall Mt. Rainier, Washington is a popular place for mountain climbing. But because of the cold, snowy winters, most people wait until summertime to grab their backpacks and ropes. Rock-climbing centers like Stone Gardens are one way to stay in shape the rest of the year.

EATS FOR KIDS Next door to Stone Gardens, try the **Lockspot Café** (3005 N.W. 54th, tel. 206/789–4865), where you can eat indoors or out, for great fish 'n' chips. Heading east, you'll find lots of interesting shops and restaurants in downtown Ballard. **The Grand Chinese Buffet** (1545 N.W. Market, tel. 206/784–8955) serves a terrific lunchtime buffet.

THE SUMMIT AT SNOQUALMIE

Just 45 minutes east of Seattle lies this fairytale land of snowy mountain peaks, alpine villages, and meadows cloaked in wildflowers. Once you get there, head for the Summit at Snoqualmie, the center for year-round mountain fun.

In the wintertime through spring, the whole family can shush down the slopes from one of six base camps. Snoqualmie has excellent lifts and the largest night-skiing area in the country. Its ski classes are renowned for their success, and kids as young as 3 can join the Mini-Mites program, which costs about $180 for five weeks of classes. While the tots are snow-plowing, Mom and Dad can hit the black diamonds from the Edelweiss lift. For children not yet ready to ski, daycare is available for babies as young as 6 months, starting at $8 an hour.

For adventure-loving tots, you can take them to the tubing hill for a ride on Mom or Dad's lap down the groomed slope. You don't even have to lug the baby back uphill;

KEEP IN MIND In the summertime, you can rent a mountain bike from CyclePath Bike & Board, right at the Summit. Bikes rent for $35 a full day, $20 a half day. Baby trailers are an extra $15, and will hold two children weighing up to a total of 80 pounds.

EATS FOR KIDS In the wintertime, the Summit abounds with restaurants and snack bars. The **Timberhouse Cafe** (2181 S.R. 906, tel. 425/434–7669) on Summit Central, serves pizza and mac-'n'-cheese. At **Webb's Restaurant & Bar** (1001 S.R. 906, Snoqualmie Pass, tel. 425/434–7669), a cafeteria on Summit West, you can dine on nearly everything from burgers to steaks. In the summertime, most of the restaurants close for the season, so your best bet is to fill that picnic basket!

1001 S.R. 906, Snoqualmie Pass

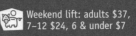 Weekend lift: adults $37, 7–12 $24, 6 & under $7

 425/434-6779; 425/434-7669; www.summit-at-snoqualmie.com

Vary; nighttime skiing available

2 and up

just hook your tube to the lift. Tubing costs about $10 per 2-hour session; $8 for children under 13. Just beside the tubing hill, children ages 6 to 12 (and under 110 pounds) can zip around a racetrack in mini-snowmobiles that travel up to 8 mph. Each 10-minute race costs $10, though, and you'll have a tough time convincing the kids that once is enough! For teens, Summit provides snowboard lessons and even classes for youths interested in becoming ski instructors.

Come springtime, the mountains shed the lower layers of their snowy coats and burst into bloom. That's the time for hiking, bicycling and just soaking in the scenery. Even the lifts transform into warm-weather mode, carrying bicyclists and their bikes up the mountain, then dropping them at the top for the fun trip downhill. If your kids are too little for steep biking trails, you can just ride up and down the lift and enjoy the view.

HEY KIDS! At one time, skiing was a lot of work. Snow-lovers used to trudge all the way up the mountain before they could take that oh-so-fast trip back down again. You might spend all day skiing but only get to come down the slope two or three times. Nowadays, skiers zip back uphill on rope tows, chair lifts, and even high-speed quads.

The Suquamish Museum takes you way back—a few thousand years or so—to a time when western Washington's towering cedars shared the forests with human inhabitants who left few footprints on the land. This Smithsonian award-winning collection shows what life was like back when cedar-hewn Suquamish Indian villages dotted the coastline across the Puget Sound from Seattle, and local tribes lived in harmony with each other and Mother Nature.

The exhibits are thoughtfully designed to draw visitors into the ancient Indian lifestyle. The basket collection shows off the intricate handiwork and describes the purpose of each: clam gathering, fish collecting, even berry-picking. Another display illustrates the extensive variety of the Native American diet, which included lots of modern favorites, plus some more exotic items. Your kids may have tried clams, oysters, salmon, crabs, huckleberries, potatoes, and onions, but they'll probably chuckle at the idea of munching on lilies or cattails.

EATS FOR KIDS Continue north on S.R. 305 along breathtaking Liberty Bay, and follow the signs to the Poulsbo city center, where you'll find an authentic Scandinavian-style village. At **Sheila's Bay Café** (18779 Front St. N.E., tel. 360/779–2997), you can sit indoors or out on the waterfront and order sandwiches, burgers or soups. **Orca North** (19045 State Highway 305 N.E., tel. 360/697–5404) serves American fare—burgers, steaks and fish—in a family-friendly atmosphere. Stop at **Sluys Poulsbo Bakery** (18924 Front St. N.E., tel. 360/779–2798) for incredible donuts, Scandinavian rosettes, and cream-filled pastries.

Older children will enjoy the pictures of 19th-century tribal life. One shows a somber Chief Seattle, snapped in 1865, a year before he died and 10 years after he signed a treaty with the U.S. government. The moving speech he is purported to have made at the time—asking for access to sacred burial grounds and predicting his people's demise—is posted at the museum, a somber but important history lesson.

The exhibits are sure to break some stereotypes for older children whose main contact with Native American culture has been via Hollywood. They can see the remnants of a proud, peaceful civilization that excelled at basket-making, canoeing, and fishing. Most of the tribe's remaining members live on Port Madison Reservation, where the museum stands, across Puget Sound from Seattle via the Bainbridge Island ferry.

KEEP IN MIND

Although the history lessons are too advanced for kids under 5, this museum is small enough and the displays colorful enough to keep younger children's attention. But keep the little ones in strollers or you may find pieces of the displays—like the smooth, pretty river rocks—tucked into their pockets when you leave.

HEY KIDS! Around 1900, Suquamish Indian children were sent away from their reservations to attend boarding schools. They learned a lot at school, but not much about their native culture. Nowadays, most Americans strive to celebrate their heritage. Whether it's Indian or Irish, it's a big part of who we are.

TILLICUM VILLAGE

9

Step onto Blake Island and you'll enter an ancient world of myth and magic—a world where Native American tribes came together for huge feasts and elaborate, colorful dances that celebrated their sacred legends. The feasts, called potlatches, were held in low, rambling log structures called longhouses, which are recreated at Tillicum Village, where a dozen Northwest tribes are represented on the staff.

Tillicum is believed to be the birthplace of Chief Seattle. You're welcomed to the island with a bowl of tender steamed clams, a favorite Native American fare. Then you can wander along the nature trails and explore the island's natural beauty. Have the kids watch out for the many animals who live here—owls, eagles, woodpeckers, and deer. Point out the open fire where huge slabs of salmon are slowly baking, just as they did centuries ago. The aroma fills the island. The dinner is served buffet-style inside the longhouse, and includes such seasonal dishes as new red potatoes and huckleberry cobbler.

GETTING THERE Drive to Piers 55 and 56 along Seattle's Central Waterfront and board the Argosy boat to Tillicum Village. Early reservations are a must in the summertime.

KEEP IN MIND Before dinner, look inside the longhouse for Alexander Joseph, resident carver and member of the Interior Salish Nation. He's usually busy carving the beautiful masks used in the after-dinner dance performances. Youngsters over 5 will enjoy watching his precise and amazingly fast knife at work. If you just have to have one of these colorful masks for your child's room, you'll find them for sale in the craft shop.

Blake Island

 $65 adult,
$25 ages 5–12

206/443–1244;
www.tillicumvillage.com

Days and times vary seasonally;
tours last 4 hours

 5 and up

The real treat comes later, when the lights go down and the dancers come on stage. The drama, color, and music draw children—and adults—into the legends, which are briefly explained before each dance. The performances, with the enormous snapping bird masks and dramatic lighting, may be a bit intense for timid preschoolers. But for brave or older children, this is a fabulous way to introduce them to an ancient culture, beautiful and yet so different from their own.

The lighting and sound effects are hardly authentic, but they add drama to the traditional dance and costumes, which remain the focus. After the show, you'll have a few minutes to browse through the handicrafts before your boat whisks you back—ready or not—to the 21st century.

HEY KIDS! While you're wandering around the island on the nature trails, keep a sharp eye out for deer. About 100 of them live on the island, and many are tame enough to come right up and beg for food. If you look behind the kitchen, you may see why—the cooks often bring out a bunch of carrots for the deer. No wonder they love people!

THE UNDERGROUND TOUR

This walk on the wacky side of the city's colorful past takes you underneath the present-day sidewalks to a honeycomb world of deserted storefronts, sidewalks, and memorabilia from the 1890s. The tour guides are part historian, part stand-up comic, and their shtick is poking fun at Seattle's wild-and-wooly founders. Since they lead special tours for school groups, they're used to keeping kids amused.

After Seattle burned down in 1889, the city decided to tackle an overdue project—leveling out the cliffs along Elliott Bay. The people who lived at the bottom of those cliffs had been having serious flooding and sewage problems for years, so the whole city needed to move up 30 feet or so above its current level. But with the Gold Rush business booming, merchants didn't want to wait around for the regrade. So they rebuilt their shops at the existing level, but when the new streets and sidewalks were added, they were much higher. Shoppers had to climb, sometimes 32 feet up a ladder, to cross the street. After

KEEP IN MIND Some of the material presented on the tour is adult-oriented, especially the discussion of Seattle's "seamstresses," an occupation listed by many local women during the Gold Rush. The implication is clear that not much sewing was going on. You might have some explaining to do to inquisitive teens, but the delicate wording will go over the heads of younger children.

608 First Ave.

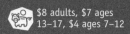 $8 adults, $7 ages 13–17, $4 ages 7–12

 Daily; times vary seasonally

206/682–4646;
www.undergroundtour.com

 7 and up

the cliffs were leveled, all the stores and hotels had to be rebuilt yet again, at the higher level, but the buildings below ground stayed.

When the shops were still operating at the lower level, opaque glass squares were installed in the sidewalks above. Your tour guide will probably stop under these squares and encourage everyone to yell "Help!" to startle passersby up above. Kids eat this up. They also love the part where the guide says cheerfully: "If you see a rat, raise your hand so everyone can scream."

The tour is great fun. With its flights of stairs, uneven flooring and 90-minute length, this is an excellent choice for older children. Strollers are not allowed, though, and you'll find no handicapped access. Portable stools, however, are available for those who need to stop and rest along the way.

HEY KIDS! Do you believe in ghosts? A few visitors to underground Seattle think they've spotted a friendly spirit floating around. You may have even seen a Scooby-Doo show with the cartoon pals chasing a ghost through Seattle's underground. So keep an eye out!

EATS FOR KIDS The Underground Café (610 1st, tel. 206/682–4646), inside the building where the tour starts, serves a variety of sandwiches and snacks. You can buy your tickets, then grab a bite while you wait for your tour to start. If you'd rather do a little exploring, walk a block up to **Walter's Waffles** (106 James St., tel. 206/382–2692), where Walter makes focaccia sandwiches like nobody's business, and throws in a chunk of his tasty, European-style waffles on the side. The ice cream waffle is a meal in itself!

VICTORIA CLIPPER

With such a friendly neighbor practically next door, a day trip to Canada is hard to resist. Victoria Clipper's boats leave early in the morning from the Seattle waterfront and arrive just two or three hours later—one vessel is faster than the other—at the British Columbia island of Victoria.

During your trip, the captain points out landmarks and relates a bit of history. To get the best view of the Olympic Mountains, sit toward the port, or left, side of the boat. If you like, you can go out on the deck later on, but hang onto your child's hands. These boats really move, so it's windy out there. In the summertime, you might just spot some killer whales leaping around the Sound. If so, the boat will slow down so you can get a good look at these graceful giants.

On nearly every trip, the crew sees some Dahl porpoises—but they're quick, so you'll need a sharp eye. Once you reach Victoria, the problem is deciding what to do. The

HEY KIDS!

You'll probably see lots of totem poles in Victoria. Some are ancient, and others have been carved to look just like the old ones. Look at the faces on the poles and try to guess who—or what—they are. They could be characters from a magical story or faces of honored tribe members.

KEEP IN MIND If you have young children, arrive early and grab a family-size table instead of the airline-style pull-downs. You'll have to stow your stroller on board. For peace and quiet, choose the upper deck, but with noisy youngsters, you might feel more comfortable below. If your kids are under 7, ask for the faster boat, the Clipper IV. It will get you there in two hours instead of three. The slower boat has no diaper-changing area.

2701 Alaskan Way, Pier 69

 206/448–5000;
www.victoriaclipper.com

 $59–$109 adults; $29.50–
$62.50 ages 1–11 (free
during non-peak months)

 Daily; departure times vary

3 and up

most popular destination is the incomparable Butchart Gardens. You can buy a Gray Line tour to the gardens through the Victoria Clipper. Butchart is a candy shop of colors, filled with sunken gardens, waterfalls, dancing fountains, and every kind of flower imaginable. There are also grassy meadows for running, and a log house for playing.

If you decide to spend the day in Victoria, you can opt for a city tour or just roam around on your own. Miniature World charms visitors with diorama-size displays of everything from railways to Mother Goose. Push a button and some of the exhibits will spring to life. At Beacon Hill Park, you'll find 150 acres of scenic oceanfront trails, ponds, and gardens to stretch those little legs before they climb back on the boat.

Too much to fit in? Overnight packages are available, but if you're traveling with a preschooler, one day is just about right.

EATS FOR KIDS At Butchart Gardens, eat sandwiches and pasta cafeteria-style at the **Blue Poppy Restaurant**. Try sweet scones and yummy finger sandwiches at **James Bay Tea Room & Restaurant** (332 Menzies St., tel. 250/382–8282). It's cozy and homelike and costs about five bucks. And on your way to Victoria, if you had to rush to leave the house, you can order a Continental breakfast on the boat for about $3. On the way back, a light dinner is about $7.

VOLUNTEER PARK

There's something for everyone at Seattle's elegant Volunteer Park, spread across 45 acres in charming Capitol Hill. For the little ones, the main attraction is the extra-large playground, crammed with lots of climbing equipment and challenging slides. A separate, roomy area caters to the tiniest tots, and the large wading pool is open from mid-June through Labor Day.

Take the kids for a walk past the manicured gardens and down one of several nature trails. Along the way, stop at the Volunteer Park Conservatory, a three-room greenhouse stocked with exotic tropical plants. Don't be surprised if your 6-year-old pretends to be on safari—it's easy to imagine an elephant or monkey coming around the banana trees. Admission is free.

Keep walking and you'll come to the Asian Art Museum. Perched on the museum's porch are two life-size camel statues dedicated to the city's children, kneeling and ready for

EATS FOR KIDS The park's open spaces make this the ideal spot for a picnic. If you want to sit down and eat, try the **Volunteer Park Market and Café** (1501 17th Ave. E., tel. 206/328–3155) for any kind of sandwich you can think of, from egg salad to curry turkey chutney. If you're in the mood for noodles, drive down to **Succulent Noodle Pan-Asian Café** (524 15th Ave., tel. 206/328–2406) or the **Olympia Pizza & Spaghetti House III** (516 15th Ave., tel. 206/329–4500). Both are tasty, reasonably priced, and child-friendly.

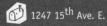 1247 15th Ave. E.

 Park free; Asian Art Museum $6, students $4, under 12 free

 Park, daily 4 AM–11:30 PM; Asian Art Museum, T–Su 10–5, Th 10–9

206/684-4743, conservatory; 206/684-7796, wading pool; 206/ 296-4232, parks department

 All ages

"riders." There's no charge to hop on! Inside, a collection of ancient pottery, china, and jewelry reflects Seattle's Asian-influenced heritage. A life-size model of a traditional Japanese home makes a perfect playhouse for younger kids. Following Japanese custom, shoes must be removed before entering, giving parents the perfect opportunity to talk to older children about cultural differences. Next to the house is an art room where youngsters can try their hand at calligraphy and other Asian crafts.

Across the street from the museum, you can't miss the huge chunk of granite erected by Spanish-American War veterans. The park is named for the volunteers who served in that war. Beyond the memorial, you'll catch a breathtaking view of the Cascades and the city skyline.

KEEP IN MIND
Stately homes, an attraction all by themselves, enrich the neighborhood immediately surrounding Volunteer Park. The park area, though perfectly safe during the day, is best avoided after dark.

HEY KIDS! Got your sneakers on? If so, and you're not afraid of heights, ask Mom or Dad if it's OK to climb the water tower. The tower, though, is taller than it looks. It will take you 106 steps to climb the 75 feet to the observation deck. Once you reach the top, you can spot the Cascade Mountains, the Space Needle, and Puget Sound.

WASHINGTON PARK ARBORETUM

Had enough shopping and museum-hopping? Time to head for the woods and enjoy some fresh air. And guess what! You don't have to leave the city. Nestled in the heart of Seattle is a magnificent 230-acre urban forest alive with birds, wildlife, and more than 20,000 trees and plants.

You can enjoy the Arboretum in lots of ways, but it's way too big to cover in one visit. Instead, pick one or two garden areas to explore, such as the Rhododendron Glen or Azalea Way. If you're really crunched for time, you can just drive through and admire the scenery, which changes dramatically through the year. Spring and fall are spectacular, but each season is rich with color and texture.

On weekends, free tours leave from the visitor center at 1 PM. You can also pick up maps of the park, self-guided tours, and lists of seasonal plants, which enable youngsters

HEY KIDS!

Way back in 1899, the city and the University of Washington wanted to create a botanical garden to show off the area's natural beauty. They started by planting 2,000 trees. Over the years, a lot more plants and trees have been added, creating the beautiful forests and gardens you see today.

KEEP IN MIND Because of its strong Asian heritage, the Northwest is rich in Japanese gardens, famous for their beauty and tranquility. Designed by Japanese garden architect Juki Iida, the garden at the south end of the Arboretum is one of the area's finest and most authentic. To give older kids a taste of Japanese culture, take them to the gardens at 1:30 PM on the third Saturday of the month for a free demonstration of the ancient tea ceremony.

2300 Arboretum Drive E.

Free

206/543-8800

Daily 7 AM to sunset

2 and up

to check off all the plants they can find. The plants are labeled throughout the park, so make it a learning game!

The best way to experience the beauty of the Arboretum is to simply get out and wander. Trails of various lengths wend their way throughout the park. A big family favorite is the Waterfront Trail, a half-mile hike along Union Bay. Starting at the north end of the Arboretum, the Waterfront Trail winds through swampy marshes and magical forests, spanning two little islands.

Along the way, the floating boardwalk is always a hit. If you have a tiny tot, a backpack carrier is a practical choice. The scenery will keep the little one entertained; and you'll be free to enjoy it, too. Plan about an hour for your walk. And when your adventure's over, civilization's just two minutes away.

EATS FOR KIDS South of the Arboretum is the Madison Park area, with lots of shops and restaurants. Great spots for kids include **Cactus Restaurant** (4220 E. Madison, tel. 206/324–4140) for Mexican food, **Café Starbucks** (4000 E. Madison, tel. 206/329–3736) for sandwiches or cookies, and **Grady's Montlake Pub & Eatery** (2307 24th E., tel. 206/726–5968) for chicken strips, macaroni and cheese, and burgers.

WASHINGTON STATE HISTORY MUSEUM

4

At this endlessly interactive museum, 20 minutes south of Seattle, kids and adults are invited to see, touch, and hear history in the making. Digging up the past is lots of fun when the facts and figures are cleverly disguised as entertainment.

Elaborate audio-visual effects and walk-through dioramas transport visitors to various eras in Washington's past to "eavesdrop" on folks describing life at the time. As kids walk through the exhibits, remind them that they're following the paths of various people who settled in the Northwest over the centuries. In the Great Hall, you'll hear stories of the Native Americans who once populated the state, and get a taste of their ancient languages. Next drop in on Lewis & Clark during their meeting with the friendly Indian leaders who led them to the mighty Columbia River. Every half-hour, you can take your own trip down the Columbia, via a three-screen video that tells of the many ways people depend on rivers for food, irrigation, energy, and transportation.

HEY KIDS! While you're visiting the museum, see if you can find the smallest and largest historic items on display. You'll need good eyesight to spot the tiniest one, since it's just a half-inch in diameter. It's a lapel pin made during the Industrial Revolution by union workers who wanted safer workplaces and better wages. The biggest item? A giant wood-cutting machine used to cut cedar logs into shingles.

1911 Pacific Ave.,
Tacoma

 $7 adult, $5
ages 6–college;
$20 family

 Spring/Summer: M, T, W, F 10–4, Th 10–8, Sa 10–5,
Su 12–5; Fall/Winter: T, W, F 10–4, Th 10–8, Sa 10–5,
Su 12–5

253/272–3500

 8 and up

The museum also includes more somber elements, such as the homeless men huddled in a Hooverville shack, discussing their plight as a Seattle rainstorm and the Great Depression raged on. What makes all these stories memorable for children is hearing them described in the "voices" of the people who lived them.

If your kids are in grade 4 through high school, stop at the History Learning Lab, a popular resource for local schools. Here's how it works: A "virtual" detective named Inspecta Detecta invites youngsters into her lab to solve various levels of historical mysteries. Kids get a question about a historical fact or figure, then embark upon a computerized search for clues. Just like real scientists, they have lots of "tools" to help them find a solution, such as old newspapers, calendars, maps and pictures. Just another sneaky way of making history fun!

GETTING THERE

Drive south on Interstate 5 to Tacoma's City Center (Exit # 133), then follow the I–705/ City Center signs to 21st St. Turn left onto 21st, then right onto Pacific Avenue. You can park in the Pacific Avenue lot or behind the museum.

EATS FOR KIDS Across the street from the museum, the kids can munch on a grilled cheese sandwich while you feast on steak and potatoes at the casual, reasonably priced **Harmon Brewing Corp. & Restaurant** (1938 Pacific Ave., tel. 253/383–2739).

WILD WAVES & ENCHANTED VILLAGE

eattle is enchanting in many ways, but it's not exactly a mecca of amusement parks or water rides. When it comes to attractions, Mother Nature usually steals the show; but when it comes to toe-dipping, the weather is usually a bit nippy. But at this park 25 minutes south of Seattle, you'll get more than your fill of both.

Carved out of a forested hillside, the park wraps around trees for a pleasantly non-concrete experience. The Enchanted Railway, atop the hill, chugs past a breath-catching overview of rides, water slides and firs. From the northern lot, you'll enter the Village through Kids' Kingdom, an unusually large section of adventures. Each ride is labeled with height requirements. Boats and carousels are for riding; ball pits and climbing equipment for exploring; a kiddie coaster for screeching; and a small Ferris wheel for soaring. But what really gets kids revved up is a motorized-car track, where mini-Marios can "race" past a cast of amusing animal characters.

EATS FOR KIDS You can bring coolers into Enchanted Village, but not to Wild Waves. So park in the north lot, go through the Village first, and dine at one of the picnic areas or on the grassy hill overlooking the lake. Alternatively, you'll find **food stands** serving pizza, hamburgers, and seafood.

HEY KIDS! Merry-go-rounds may not be quite as spine-tingling as the corkscrew roller coaster, but something about them makes almost everyone want to hop on board. People have felt that way about merry-go-rounds, or carousels, as they're also called, since the turn of the 20th century. Between 1890 and 1925, 10,000 carousels' worth of hand-carved horses went galloping, snorting, and charging around amusement parks across the United States. Today, only about 140 of those old wooden carousels remain. The one at Enchanted Village was built in 1906.

36201 Enchanted Parkway
South, Federal Way

 253/661-8029

$25 adult; $21
children under 48";
free 2 & under

 late May–mid-Jun, M–F 9:30–4:30,
Sa–Su 10–6; mid Jun–Labor Day,
daily 10–6 (Village), 11–7 (Waves)

1 and up

More fun ensues for older kids, with a giant Gunnysack slide (you can hold a tot on your lap), an adrenalin-pumping Wild Thing corkscrew coaster, and the usual assortment of other rides that turn you upside down and inside-out. If younger kids are fading by the time you hit Wild Waves, rent a stroller at the stand with the locker keys. (Changing rooms are uphill from the lockers). Hopefully, your little swimmers will revive long enough for a dip in Kids Splash Central, with its fountains, mini-tube rides, and gentle slides.

Older kids will happily splash the afternoon away in the giant wave pool, the wild Konga River ride, and on the turbulent tube rides. They'll find plenty of slides—speed slides, drop slides, cannonball slides, and even a super-duper corkscrew. If you have little ones, you can take them to the 2-foot-deep toddler pool on the Village side, complete with sprinkler and slides.

Everybody goes home tired and happy. Now, that's real enchantment!

KEEP IN MIND The admission price includes two complete parks. Be aware, however, that a few of the activities cost extra. The remote-control boats, video machines, and shooting gallery require spare change; the paddle boats cost $4 per half hour; and the sky-dive bungee jump is $30 for up to three riders.

WING LUKE ASIAN MUSEUM

Asian immigrants have played a significant role in shaping our country's history, particularly the Pacific Northwest. At this museum, colorful exhibits tell the tales of a wide variety of groups: Hawaiians, Chinese, Japanese, Koreans, Filipinos, South and Southeast Asians, Cambodians, Laotians, Vietnamese.

The permanent exhibit "One Song, Many Voices" tells about the migration, starting 200 years ago, of Asians to the United States. Through photos and items donated by the Asian-American community, kids can see how the immigrants built their new lives—by working on the railroads, in lumber camps and sawmills, canning salmon, farming, and opening such businesses as restaurants and laundries.

Some exhibits will require an explanation and contemplation, such as the gripping "Camp Harmony," which is a model of an internment camp where Japanese Americans

HEY KIDS! Giant dragon and lion kites are colorful and fun to watch, but they're also important symbols in many Asian cultures. The dragon stands for strength, and the lion stands for wisdom and peace. Both are thought to bring good luck. During the Chinese New Year, lion kites are pulled through the streets, and the lion "dances" in front of homes and businesses. To thank the lion for good luck to come, people leave lettuce on their doorsteps for their honored guest to "eat."

 407 Seventh Ave. S.

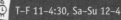 206/623-4990;
www.wingluke.org

 $4 adult,
$2 ages 5–12

T-F 11–4:30, Sa-Su 12–4

 8 and up

were confined during World War II. Barbed wire surrounds the "camp," which includes a replica of a cattle stall converted into living quarters for a whole family. Wartime music, radio broadcasts from the era, and the voices of former internees describing their experience enhance the experience.

If you have older teens who are fascinated by this history, they may enjoy the Wing Luke's computerized recordings of Japanese Americans describing their lives before, during, and after World War II. There are two computer workstations, available during museum hours and after hours by appointment.

Remember to guide the kids to the 35-foot-long Chinese dragon hanging from the ceiling, the fanciful animal kites, and the dragon racing boat.

KEEP IN MIND
The International District is not a high-crime area at any time of day, but it's best at night to park close to your destination and stay in lighted areas.

EATS FOR KIDS Cheap, scrumptious food isn't hard to find in the International District. You can get a tasty barbecue chicken, pork, or duck lunch-box to go at **King's Barbecue House** (518 6th Ave. S., tel. 206/622-2828). At **Yummy House Bakery** (522 S. 6th St., tel. 206/340-9308) you can have a cup of tea, then treat the family to a slice of Chinese fruit-filled cake.

WOODLAND PARK ZOO

At this top-notch urban zoo, you'll find animals of every stripe, spot, color, and size. Woodland Park has pioneered some major trends in modern zoos, including the idea of grouping animals by regional habitat instead of species. This gives older children a much better snapshot of how these animals live in the wild.

In the African Savanna, giraffes, hippos, zebras and lions roam the grasslands—with the big cats safely ensconced in their own section. The tropical Rainforest is home to ocelots, lemurs, and birds, plus Woodland Park's world-famous gorilla habitat, for which Dian Fossey of *Gorillas in the Mist* served as a consultant. Even more exotic is the Trail of Vines, starring Malaysian tapirs, Indian pythons, and orangutans. Native Northwest critters are the stars of the Northern Trail, which includes a bear cave, bald eagle-viewing post, and underwater viewing of grizzlies and otters.

But the zoo's pride and joy—and the favorite stop for kids—is in the Tropical Asia

HEY KIDS!

While you're at the zoo, don't miss the Komodo Dragons. They can grow up to 10 feet long, which makes them the world's largest lizards. And they have very, very sharp teeth—up to 200 of them. But don't worry; they're safely locked away behind glass walls.

KEEP IN MIND Bundle up the tots in their PJs to join Mom or Dad for a Bedtime Story Safari, with a visit to the animals, followed by stories and snacks. Year-round, kids age 7 and up can go on an overnight weekend adventure with their parents. You'll walk around the zoo to watch the animals settling in for the night—or waking up—then "camp out" on the Education Center's carpeted floor. In the morning, you can watch the critters start their day.

exhibit. The park's first-ever baby elephant, Hansa, weighed in at a cuddly 235 pounds when she was born in late 2000. Youngsters and parents alike will identify with her persistent efforts to get Mom to play with balls and sticks! Tucked away but not-to-be-missed is the Family Farm petting zoo, a highlight for toddlers but popular with older kids, too. After they commune with the critters, elementary-age children can enjoy crafts and activities in the Discovery Barn. The Family Farm is open May through October.

Summertime brings pony rides and the Butterflies & Blooms exhibit, which enchants visitors with its 1,000 or so fluttering residents. Even in the wintertime, you can view Puget Sound native butterflies in the permanent Bug World exhibit, which they share with a variety of endearing occupants such as earwigs, tarantulas, and scorpions.

All the exhibits are designed with strollers in mind. It's hard to think of a better place to spend the day; you'll have plenty to see.

EATS FOR KIDS If you're having way too much fun to leave the zoo, make a quick stop at the zoo's **Rain Forest Café** (tel. 206/684–4800) for a pizza or sandwich. In Fremont, try a variety of comfort fare from waffles to creative pastas at the **Longshoreman's Daughter** (3508 Fremont Place N., tel. 206/633–5169).

CLASSIC GAMES

"I SEE SOMETHING YOU DON'T SEE AND IT IS BLUE." Stuck for a way to get your youngsters to settle down in a museum? Sit them down on a bench in the middle of a room and play this vintage favorite. The leader gives just one clue—the color—and everybody guesses away.

"I'M GOING TO THE GROCERY..." The first player begins, "I'm going to the grocery and I'm going to buy... " and finishes the sentence with the name of an object, found in grocery stores, that begins with the letter "A." The second player repeats what the first player has said, and adds the name of another item that starts with "B." The third player repeats everything that has been said so far and adds something that begins with "C" and so on through the alphabet. Anyone who skips or misremembers an item is out (or decide up front that you'll give hints to all who need 'em). You can modify the theme depending on where you're going that day, as "I'm going to X and I'm going to see..."

FAMILY ARK Noah had his ark—here's your chance to build your own. It's easy: just start naming animals and work your way through the alphabet, from antelope to zebra.

PLAY WHILE YOU WAIT

NOT THE GOOFY GAME Have one child name a category. (Some ideas: first names, last names, animals, countries, friends, feelings, foods, hot or cold things, clothing.) Then take turns naming things that fall into that category. You're out if you name something that doesn't belong in the category—or if you can't think of another item to name. When only one person remains, start again. Choose categories depending on where you're going or where you've been—historic topics if you've seen a historic sight, animal topics before or after the zoo, upside-down things if you've been to the circus, and so on. Make the game harder by choosing category items in A-B-C order.

DRUTHERS How do your kids really feel about things? Just ask. "Would you rather eat worms or hamburgers? Hamburgers or candy?" Choose serious and silly topics—and have fun!

BUILD A STORY "Once upon a time there lived..." Finish the sentence and ask the rest of your family, one at a time, to add another sentence or two. Bring a tape recorder along to record the narrative—and you can enjoy your creation again and again.

GOOD TIMES GALORE

WIGGLE & GIGGLE Give your kids a chance to stick out their tongues at you. Start by making a face, then have the next person imitate you and add a gesture of his own—snapping fingers, winking, clapping, sneezing, or the like. The next person mimics the first two and adds a third gesture, and so on.

JUNIOR OPERA During a designated period of time, have your kids sing everything they want to say.

THE QUIET GAME Need a good giggle—or a moment of calm to figure out your route? The driver sets a time limit and everybody must be silent. The last person to make a sound wins.

THE A-LIST

BEST IN TOWN
Olympic Game Farm
Pacific Science Center
Pike Place Market
Seattle Children's Theatre
Woodland Park Zoo

BEST OUTDOORS
Alki Beach Park

BEST CULTURAL ACTIVITY
Northwest Puppet Center

BEST MUSEUM
The Children's Museum

WACKIEST
Space Needle

NEW & NOTEWORTHY
History Learning Lab at the Washington State History Museum

SOMETHING FOR EVERYONE

ART ATTACK
Nordic Heritage Museum, **38**
Northwest Puppet Center, **36**
Rosalie Whyel Museum of Doll Art, **25**
Seattle Art Museum, **23**
Suquamish Museum, **10**
Tillicum Village, **9**
Wing Luke Asian Museum, **2**

COOL 'HOODS
Alki Beach Park, **68**
Bainbridge Island Historical Museum, **67**
International District, **48**
Port Gamble Historic Museum, **27**
The Underground Tour, **8**

CULTURE CLUB
Nordic Heritage Museum, **38**
Pacific Rim Bonsai Collection, **32**
Suquamish Museum, **10**
Tillicum Village, **9**
Wing Luke Asian Museum, **2**

FARMS & ANIMALS
Cougar Mountain Zoological Park, **59**
Evergreen Alpaca Farm, **57**
Lake Forest Park, **46**
Northwest Trek, **35**
Olympic Game Farm, **33**
Point Defiance Zoo & Aquarium, **28**
Remlinger Farms, **26**
The Seattle Aquarium, **24**
Woodland Park Zoo, **1**

FOOD FIXATION
International District, **48**
Pike Place Market, **29**
Remlinger Farms, **26**
Tillicum Village, **9**

FREEBIES
Alki Beach Park, **68**
Burke-Gilman Trail, **65**
Carkeek Park, **62**
Green Lake Park, **51**
International District, **48**

SOMETHING FOR EVERYONE

ALL AROUND TOWN

MANY THANKS

I am deeply indebted to the irrepressible Molly for opening my eyes to new worlds of adventures, and to Scott, who shared the fun, for his unflagging encouragement and enthusiasm. The patience and support of my editor, William Travis, are also greatly appreciated.

the end.